Knit This Doll!

9/11

Violet

Seamus

Sydney

Jonathan

Antoinette

Nicki

Milo

Max

Greg

Judith

Tabitha

Angelica

Knit This Doll!

A Step-by-Step Guide to Knitting Your Own Customizable Amigurumi Doll

By Nicki Moulton

WILEY

Wiley Publishing, Inc.

Knit This Doll!: A Step-by-Step Guide to Knitting Your Own Customizable Amigurumi Doll

Published by Wiley Publishing, Inc., Hoboken, New Jersey
Published simultaneously in Canada

For general information on our other products and services or to obtain technical support please contact our Customer Care Department within the U.S. at (877) 762-2974, outside the U.S. at (317) 572-3993 or fax (317) 572-4002.

Wiley also publishes its books in a variety of electronic formats. Some content that appears in print may not be available in electronic books. For more information about Wiley products, please visit our web site at www.wiley.com.

Library of Congress Control Number: 2011921780

ISBN: 978-0-470-62440-1 (pbk)
ISBN: 978-0-470-92252-1 (ebk)

Printed in the United States of America

10 9 8 7 6 5 4 3 2 1

Book production by Wiley Publishing, Inc. Composition Services

Note to the Readers:
Due to differing conditions, tools and the individual skills, John Wiley & Sons, Inc. assumes no responsibility for any damages, injuries suffered, or losses incurred as a result of following the information published in this book. Before beginning any project, review the instructions carefully, and if any doubts or questions remain, consult local experts or authorities. Because codes and regulations vary greatly, you always should check with authorities to ensure that your project complies with all applicable local codes and regulations. Always read and observe all of the safety precautions provided by manufacturers of any tools, equipment, or supplies, and follow all accepted safety procedures.

Nicki Moulton's original patterns are intended for non-commercial, personal use only and may not be used in the production of goods for sale in any quantity.

Credits

Senior Editor
Roxane Cerda

Senior Project Editor
Donna Wright

Technical Editor
Sharon Turner

Copy Editor
Marylouise Wiack

Editorial Manager
Christina Stambaugh

Publisher
Cindy Kitchel

Vice President and Executive Publisher
Kathy Nebenhaus

Interior Design
Lissa Auciello-Brogan

Cover Design
José Almaguer

Photography
Jodi Bratch

For Greg, who will always have my heart,
no matter how far apart we are.

Acknowledgments

None of this would have been possible if it wasn't for a suggestion from my sister, Michelle Timian, that I try finding an agent to publish my knitted doll patterns instead of just selling them online. Without her advice, encouragement and support, this book never would have happened. I have endless amounts of gratitude for her.

My husband, Greg, deserves more words of thanks than I could express. We have lived one incredible and crazy journey together, and my continued creativity is a product of his love.

My mom, who first got me into knitting, always encouraged me to keep developing my craft and never hesitated to help me build my yarn stash! Without those first knitting instructions, this book never would have happened.

My agent, Kate Epstein, has been so extraordinarily helpful through this exciting path of getting my first book published! She has been the most wonderful advocate for me, and I always ended my conversations with her feeling like a million bucks.

Roxane Cerda and Donna Wright at Wiley were absolutely the most wonderful editors a person could ask to work with. Sometimes I wondered if their enthusiasm for this project rivaled my own. They were always on call to answer my questions and doubts and made the process of book publication a joy.

Last but certainly not least, I must give immense amounts of recognition to my technical editor, Sharon Turner, who had the Olympian task of setting my patterns—most of which were little more than oddly abbreviated notes to myself—into a legible format that anyone could read. If you got through this book and completed a doll, it's all thanks to her talent.

Table of Contents

Introduction

I have always had a love/hate relationship with dolls. When my mom used to give me dolls as a child, I would constantly try to modify them to fit characters I made up. I'd cut off their hair, rip up their clothes . . . even try to draw on them. This tended to frustrate both me and my mom—my efforts never gave me the doll I wanted and my mom spent a fortune on toys that I ended up destroying. I loved my dolls, but I never found a doll that fit *exactly* what I had in mind.

It wasn't until I picked up knitting that I realized that, with a little creativity, I could create anything I wanted—even dolls. After years of developing my own patterns, I can show you how to create your own dolls as well.

The format of this book might be unlike anything you've seen before. It's not a static book of patterns where I tell you which character I think you should knit, but one that will encourage you to explore your own creativity by picking and choosing from different options (or menus) in this book. Instead of *one* pattern with instructions on how to make *one* thing, there are a whole slew of patterns that you can mix-and-match to make *anyone* you want.

And as crazy as it might seem, every doll in this book is based on the Basic Doll Pattern (starting on page 2). You don't *have* to start with the Basic Doll Pattern—you can build your own doll by jumping from menu to menu. But if you get lost or confused,

Jonathan
Head with hair template, p. 54
Hairstyle, p. 55
Hand with fingers, p. 71
V-neck sweater, p. 40
Stripes, p. 43
Jeans, p. 30
Messenger bag, p. 104
Sneakers, p. 13

My doll is going to have...

_____ feet, found on page _____

_____ legs, found on page _____

_____ torso, found on page _____

_____ face, found on page _____

_____ arms, found on page _____

_____ extras, found on page _____

you can use the illustrated step-by-step instructions to get your bearings. The Basic Doll Pattern also doesn't include any modifications, so if you would like to knit an animal or even design your own, you have a nice blank pattern to work from. So you might be asking yourself, "how do I begin?" Before jumping to page 1 with your needles ready to knit, flip through the book first. Get an idea of what kinds of options there are and start thinking about what you'd like to make. Think of this as a knitting "choose-your-own-adventure." Do you want to knit a doll wearing a turtleneck with jeans and snow boots? Or maybe a punk rocker with ripped jeans, combat boots and a Mohawk? Jot down your plans on the "Keeping Track!" form on the page, so you always know where you'll need to go for the next step of your project.

Don't worry about getting lost or confused; each menu contains a lot of photographs and charts that will guide you along the way.

So flip through the following pages, plan your pattern, grab your needles and gather your yarn, and get ready to make your own very own unique doll. Knit on!

Tips on Choosing Yarns

If you are used to typical knitting books that list exactly what brands and colors of yarns you should use, I'm sorry, but I am going to disappoint you. This section on choosing yarns might be the first and last time I mention yarn.

There's a reason for this: this book is designed for you to be as creative as you want to be. I have left it up to you to decide what brands, styles, and colors of yarn you want to knit with. There may be times when I suggest a color (white being the bottom of a sneaker), but even those aren't rules; they are only guidelines.

Here's the nitty gritty: All the patterns shown are knitted with worsted weight yarn. I personally adored Knit Picks' Wool of the Andes and Cascade 220 Wool (how can you argue with that many colors?). If you don't like wool or are allergic to it, you can use acrylic or cotton yarn, as long as you pick a worsted weight. It's also a good idea to have all of the colors you'll need on hand before you begin. The menus are a great way to use leftover yarn from other knitting projects.

Now that I've covered choosing yarn, here are some more recommendations:

Skin Tones

Skin tones may be one of the hardest things to find in a yarn shop. I have found a few great colors that I've listed here. You're free to find your own, of course, but if I could impart one bit of advice—*please* don't use white for a skin color. A very small number of people have a skin tone that is actually white. Even pale people have a bit of color. White yarn just looks tacky in my opinion, and you can do so much more with one of the following options.

- Cascade 220 Sand and Beige are wonderful, light skin tones.
- Wool of the Andes Chocolate is an absolutely beautiful, rich brown. One of my favorites!
- Wool of the Andes Snickerdoodle is a great "tanned" color.

Some Specialty Yarns

- For a set of wings for your angel, I highly recommend Bernat "Boa" yarn. It is wonderful soft and feather like, and will give you a texture. One 110-yard ball is enough for a pair of wings.
- Mermaid fins can be knitted with any worsted weight yarn, but using Berroco's Zen will give it a more "scale" like appearance. You only need one 110-yard ball in any color.

Tools

You'll need the following supplies to knit your doll:

- U.S. Size 7 (4.5mm) double-pointed needles—two sets (wood, metal, or plastic).
- Yarn. Make sure that you have enough for your project. The entire Basic Doll Pattern requires 220 yards of yarn, excluding any extras. This means that if you want to knit an all-white cat, for example, you should plan ahead and buy extra white yarn for the tail and ears. For dolls with clothing, one 220-yard ball of yarn will be adequate for each color you are using—in fact you *will* end up with extra. Using scrap yarn is totally acceptable, too, especially for smaller parts of the doll such as shoes or stripes. Use your best judgment when using choosing scrap yarn so that you will have enough to finish the project.
- Size 18mm plastic eyes. They are also sometimes offered at yarn shops and crafting stores. *Do not* use plastic eyes for a doll you intend to give to a child under the age of three—in this instance, plan on embroidering on the eyes with yarn or thread.
- Fiber fill. My personal favorite is Polyfil. It's hypoallergenic and also washable—a plus if you're planning on giving your doll to a child.
- Stitch markers (at least 10)
- Yarn needle
- Size H (5mm) crochet hook. You will need this to add hair.
- Scissors
- Black embroidery floss or yarn for embroidering facial expressions

A Word About Gauge

My gauge for a square inch is about 5 stitches by 7 rows, but I have to emphasize that gauge is not that important when making dolls. Because you're not making something for someone to wear, if your doll ends up a little bigger or a little smaller, no one is really going to notice. All the clothes and accessories are knitted as well, so as long as your tension for knitting the doll and knitting the removable accessories remains the same, everything will fit together.

Another thing to keep in mind is that the stitch counts are uniform throughout *Knit This Doll*. Which is a reason to celebrate, especially if math isn't your forte.

Even though the gauge can be flexible, remember that *maintaining an even gauge is vital!* You don't want the legs to be bigger than the torso . . . or the head to be too small for the body. Check your gauge periodically throughout your project to make sure that you are always knitting with even tension.

Basic Doll Pattern

All the patterns in this book start from the Basic Doll Pattern; every shoe is based on the basic doll's foot, and every T-shirt and sweater is an adaptation of the basic doll's torso. This means that it's not necessary to start your doll-making adventure here, but it might help you to glance over these instructions before you begin. This section is a great resource if you get stuck. The step-by-step illustrations can help you out if you can't visualize what you're supposed to do next, and the lack of instructions on where to change colors is a wonderful "blank slate" for you to be as imaginative as you want—just in case you can't find a pattern here for what you'd really like to create.

Violet

Feet

Variations for footwear patterns can be found in the Feet Menu starting on page 10.

CO 6 sts in the desired color.

Divide evenly onto three dpns, pm, and join to begin knitting in the round.

Set-up rnd: *K1, m1; rep from * around. You should end up with 4 sts on each of the three dpns (A; 12 sts total).

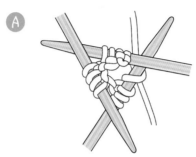

Rnd 1: Knit.

Rnd 2: *K1, m1, rep from * around (24 sts).

Rnds 3 and 4: Knit.

Rnd 5: *K1, m1, rep from * around (48 sts).

Rnds 6–11: Knit.

Rnd 12: K23, pm, k2tog, k14, k2tog, pm, k7 (B). There should be 30 sts outside of the markers (46 sts).

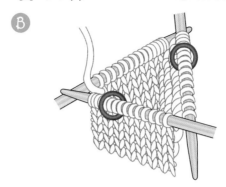

Repeat Rnd 12 until there are 2 sts left between the markers (32 sts).

Next rnd: K22, [k2tog] twice (C). You'll have to remove the markers to do this, k6 (30 sts).

Next 5 rnds: Knit. Do not break yarn unless your leg variation will require a change.

Legs

Variations for leg patterns can be found in the Legs Menu and in the Pants, Shorts, and Skirts Menu starting on pages 10 and 22.

For the basic doll, continuing from the foot, knit 31 rounds.

Leaving the 30 stitches on your needles, break off about 4 inches of yarn. Set aside. Make the second foot and leg identical to the first, but do not break the working yarn for the second leg—you'll be using it to join the legs.

Join the Legs

The placement of your doll's crotch will vary based on your tension and can even vary every time you knit a doll.

Take the legs one by one and, with the toes still pointing forward, line up a needle along the inside of each leg and determine where the "middle" of the inside of the leg lies (A). It does not matter which foot you use as the right and as the left. Place a marker at this middle point (B).

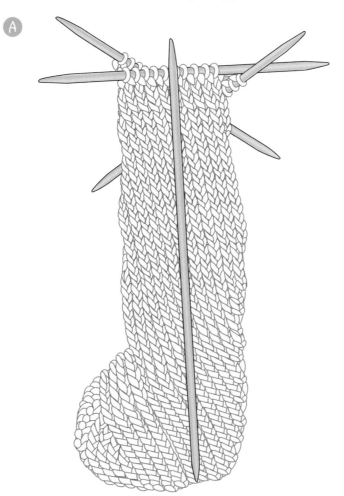

A

Place both legs side-by-side with the toes pointing forward, as you would the feet on the finished doll (C).

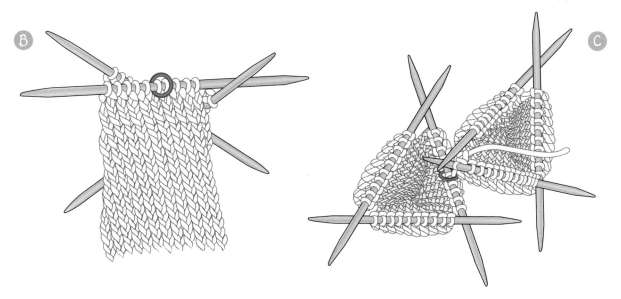

Using the working yarn left on the last leg you made, begin knitting around the leg. When you get to the marker, begin knitting the stitches from the other leg, starting at the marker you placed. Knit all 60 stitches of both legs, joining the two legs together so that you create one continuous loop (D).

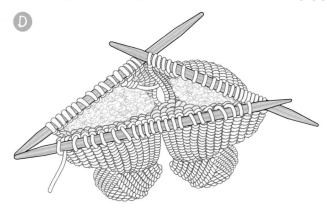

Next 9 rnds: Knit. Do not break the yarn unless your torso variation requires a change.

Before continuing with the torso, first sew the crotch and stuff the legs: Sew the crotch together back to front using the tail yarn from the first leg. Weave in the loose end. Stuff the legs.

Torso

Variations for torso patterns can be found in the Torso Menu starting on page 36.

For the basic doll, continue as follows from where you left off after the 9 knit rounds.

Rnds 1–15: Knit.

Rnd 16: *K8, k2tog, rep from * to end (54 sts).

Rnds 17–25: Knit.

Rnd 26: *K7, k2tog, rep from * to end (48sts).

Rnds 27–30: Knit.

Rnd 31: *K4, k2tog, rep from * to end (40 sts).

Rnds 32–34: Knit.

Rnd 35: *K2, k2tog, rep from * to end (30 sts). This is the neck.

Rnds 36–38: Knit.

Rnd 39 (begin head shaping): *K2, m1, rep from * to end (45 sts).

Rnd 40: Knit.

Rnd 41: *K3, m1, rep from * to end (60 sts).

Head and Face

Variations for head and face patterns can be found in the Head and Face Menu starting on page 52.

For the basic doll, continue from where you left off as follows (60 sts).

Rnds 1–16: Knit.

Rnd 17: *K4, k2tog, rep from * to end (50 sts).

Rnd 18: Knit.

Stuff the body and head. Place the eyes by inserting the protruding part from the back of the plastic safety eye into the face (A). Where you place the eyes is up to you. Placing them low on the face and wide apart will create more of the Japanese "chibi" look, while placing them in the middle of the face with about 12 stitches in between the eyes will create a more American doll look. Make sure the eyes are centered correctly on the face before securing. Secure the eyes by fastening them on the wrong side of the face (A) with the plastic or metal washer (C).

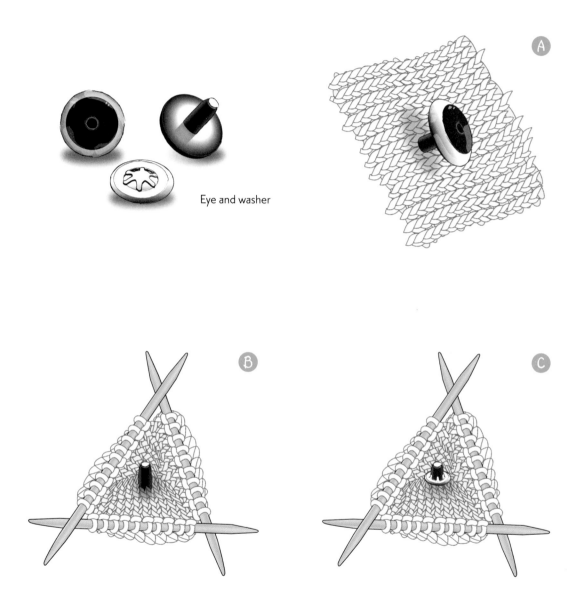

Eye and washer

A

B

C

Shape Top of Head

Rnd 19: *K3, k2tog, rep from * to end (40 sts).

Rnd 20: Knit.

Rnd 21: *K2, k2tog, rep from * to end (30 sts).

Rnd 22: Knit.

Rnd 23: *K1, k2tog, rep from * to end (20 sts).

Rnd 24: Knit.

Rnd 25: *K2tog, rep from * to end (10 sts).

Break off the tail yarn and use the tail yarn to close up the stitches. Weave in the end.

Hands

Variations for hand patterns can be found in the Hand and Arm Menu starting on page 68.

CO 10 sts, leaving a 2-inch tail.

Divide sts as evenly as possible onto three dpns, pm, and join to begin knitting in the round.

Rnd 1: Knit.

Rnd 2: *K2, m1; rep from * to end (15 sts).

Rnds 3–7: Knit.

Rnd 8 (shape wrist): *K3, k2tog; rep from * two times (12 sts).

Arms

Variations for arm patterns can be found in the Hand and Arm Menu starting on page 68.

For the basic doll, continue with the arms as follows (12 sts).

Rnds 1–5: Knit.

Rnd 6: K3, m1, k6, m1, k3 (14 sts).

Rnds 7–16: Knit.

Rnd 17: K3, m1, k8, m1, k3 (16 sts).

Rnds 18–32: Knit.

Rnd 33: **K2tog, knit to last 2 sts, k2tog (14 sts).

From here, begin working back and forth in rows.

Rnd 34: Turn and purl.**

Rep from ** to ** until 8 sts rem. BO and leave a long tail. Knit a second hand and arm to match the first.

Stuff the hands and arms. Sew each arm onto the body by first pinning the arm onto the torso, making sure both arms are centered correctly. Using the tails left at bind-off, sew the arms onto the body. Weave in any remaining loose ends.

Feet Menu

So you've flipped through the book, developed a game plan, and are all set to start knitting your very own doll? Fantastic! Welcome to the wonderful adventure of knitting your very own customizable doll! You will want to start here—with the feet. (I guess you can say that your doll will be knitted "from the ground up".) With eight patterns to choose from, you are well on your way to making a doll that is all your own.

Daisy

Plain Shoes

Sometimes you need a basic canvas to jump-start your creativity. The plain shoe pattern is just that—the bare-bones basic pattern for knitting a pair of shoes for your doll. Everything else is up to you. Add intarsia wherever you want (see page 16).

Sole

CO 6 sts in the color you want for the sole of your shoe. Divide the 6 sts evenly over three dpns. Place a marker and join in the round.

Rnd 1: *K1, m1; rep from * to end of rnd (12 sts).

Rnd 2: Knit.

Rnd 3: Work as for Rnd 1 (24 sts).

Rnds 4 and 5: Knit.

Rnd 6: Work as for Rnd 1 (48 sts).

Rnd 7 (arrange sts over four dpns): Retaining marker to indicate beg and end of rnd, k16 onto first needle (back of foot); k12 onto second needle (side of foot); k8 onto third needle (toe); k12 onto fourth needle (side of foot). Using four dpns is optional; it can help you envision the foot, but three needles can do just as well if you prefer.

Rnds 8–10: Knit. Break off yarn.

Top of Shoe

Change to the color you would like for the top of the shoe (MC).

Rnds 11–13: Knit.

Rnd 14 (set-up for toe shaping): K23, pm, k2tog, k14, k2tog, pm, k7 (46 sts total, with 16 sts between the 2 new markers).

Rnd 15: K23, sm, k2tog, knit to 2 sts before next marker, k2tog, sm, k7 (44 sts). Rep Rnd 15 until there are 2 sts rem between the markers (32 sts).

Next rnd: K22, [k2tog] twice (you'll have to remove the toe markers to do this), k6 (30 sts).

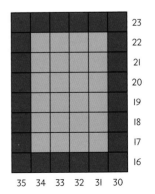

For a "low top" shoe, knit 1 more round in MC, change to the sock/skin tone and knit 5 rounds, then continue to the leg pattern. For a "high top" shoe, knit 5 more rounds in MC, then continue to the Legs Menu.

Rnd 17 (for light-blue striped tongue): K30, change to CC and k4. Change to MC, finish row. Rep pattern for 6 rows.

Knit the second shoe identical to the first.

Sneakers

Ever since the original design burst into the sports scene in 1917, the Chuck Taylor brand has become the footwear of choice for everyone from jocks to nerds to rockers. You'll need to use two different colors of yarn and a bit of intarsia (see page 16) to knit up a pair of these kicks inspired by the "Chuck Ts". Timeless fashion doesn't come any cooler than this.

Sole

Rnds 1–10: Using white (W), work as for plain shoes (48 sts).

Top of Shoe

Rnd 11: Change to the color you would like for the top of the shoe (MC). K24 in MC, k16 in W, knit rem 8 sts in MC.

Rnds 12 and 13: Knit rounds as established in Rnd 11.

Rnd 14: K23 in MC, pm; in W, k2tog, k14, k2tog, pm, k7 in MC (46 sts total, with 16 sts between the 2 new markers).

Rnd 15: K23 in MC, sm; using W, k2tog, knit to 2 sts before next marker, k2tog, sm; k7 in MC (44 sts).

Rnds 16–18: Rep Rnd 15 until there are 8 W sts rem. Break off W and continue knitting only in MC (38 sts). Rep Rnd 15 until there are 2 sts rem between the markers (32 sts).

Next rnd: Using MC only, k22, [k2tog] twice (you'll have to remove the toe markers to do this), k6 (30 sts).

For a "low top" shoe, knit 1 more round in MC, change to the sock/skin tone and knit 5 rnds, then continue to the leg pattern. For a "high top" shoe, knit 5 more rounds in MC, then continue to the Legs Menu.

Knit the second shoe identical to the first.

Combat Boots

Although they stand at two ends of the political spectrum, soldiers and punks can both agree on what goes on their feet. Combat boots are legendary for being tough, resilient, and durable—these simple-to-knit versions will make your doll ready for anything! They are a snap to make and a little extra embroidery will add that classic punk feel.

Sole

Rnds 1–10: Using brown, work as for the plain shoe (48 sts).

Top of Boot

Change to black.

Rnd 11–13: Knit.

Rnd 14: K23, pm, k2tog, k14, k2tog, pm, k7 (46 sts, with 16 sts between the markers).

Rnd 15: K23, sm, k2tog, knit to 2 sts before next marker, k2tog, sm, k7 (44 sts).

Rep Rnd 15 until there are 2 sts rem between the markers (32 sts).

Next rnd: K22, [k2tog] twice (you'll have to remove the toe markers to do this), k6 (30 sts).

Knit 5 more rounds in black, then continue to the Legs Menu.

Knit a second boot identical to the first.

For extra detail, thread a needle with a bright-colored thread and embroider stitches around the bottom of the boot.

Cowboy Boots

Independent, free, and filled with wanderlust—cowboy boots, as well as the cowboys and cowgirls who wear them, represent an iconic image of Americana that is easily recognized around the world. These knitted versions are first knit in the round and then divided into two halves that are knitted flat. Complete the look by knitting a pair of legs in a skin tone or denim and sew the boots over them. Round up your needles and get to it, partner!

Sole

Rnds 1–10: Using the color you would like the sole to be, work as for the plain shoes (48 sts).

Top of Boot

Change to the color you would like for the top of the boot (MC).

Rnds 11–14: K23, pm, k2tog, k14, k2tog, pm, k7 (46 sts, with 16 sts between the markers).

Rnd 15: K23, sm, k2tog, knit to 2 sts before next marker, k2tog, sm, k7 (44 sts).

Rep Rnd 15 until there are 4 sts rem between the markers (34 sts).

Now that the toe is finished, you can make the boot as short or tall as you'd like. If you prefer a shorter boot, continue from here. If you prefer a taller boot, knit 10 more rounds before moving on to the next step.

Note: From here, the shaft of the boot is divided and the two halves are worked back and forth in rows, one side at a time.

Next row (RS): K8, turn.

Row 2 (WS): K2tog, p13, k2tog, turn. (Leave the rem 17 sts on holder for later.)

Row 3: K2tog, knit to last 2 sts, k2tog.

Working Intarsia in the Round?

There are a few patterns in this book that call for the use of intarsia in the round. You might read that and think, "But I can't do intarsia in the round!" Have no fear! Here are three different methods you can use:

1 **Float On:** Knit the first round that calls for intarsia as you normally would if your piece were knitted flat. When you complete the first row of intarsia, twist together the main color yarn with the contrast color yarn and complete the round. When you get to the second row of intarsia, make a *very* loose float to the beginning of the row ("very loose" means go crazy with it). Remember that the inside of your doll is going to get filled with stuffing, so no one is going to notice the floats. Twist the main color yarn with the contrast color yarn and knit the row of intarsia. You should only use this method for smaller intarsia designs. Alternatively, you can also use a duplicate stitch for smaller intarsia designs.

2 **Flat Again:** When you get to a point in your doll pattern that calls for intarsia, switch from knitting in the round to knitting flat. Work the first round of your intarsia pattern as you normally would if you were knitting flat. When you get to the end of the round, turn the work and purl the next row—just like knitting flat! Continue to knit one row, purl one row in stockinette stitch until you are done with your color pattern. When you complete your intarsia, return to knitting in the round and seam the rows you knitted flat.

3 **Cutting and Joining:** When you join a new contrast color yarn to work in intarsia, cut the main color yarn. Work to the end of the intarsia row, cut the contrast color yarn and rejoin the main color yarn. Make sure to tie together the loose ends of the yarn with a knot. Continue in this manner until the intarsia chart is complete. With this method, it is *very* important to go back and seam together where you joined the two colors because the knots can poke out from between the stitches.

Row 4: K2tog, purl to last 2 sts, k2tog.

Rep last 2 rows until there are 7 sts rem. BO.

Rejoin the yarn to the 17 sts on the holder, ready to work a WS row and work Rows 2–4 (on the previous page).

Work the second boot identical to the first.

Using a contrasting color, thread a needle and sew details into the boot. You can simply stitch around the toe, following the decreased sts from earlier. You can also knit around the top of the boot, embroider a design onto the sides . . . anything you want.

When you move to the Legs Menu, CO 30 sts instead of continuing with 30 sts. Attach the cowboy boot by stuffing the legs into the boot, and sew them together.

Mary Janes

Sweet and innocent or devilishly fashionable? This classic shoe successfully conjures images of both sensible schoolgirls and modern haute fashion. Don't let the intarsia and separately knitted strap discourage you from testing your skills—your doll will look either cute-as-a-button or tough-as-nails with these on her feet.

Flats Variation: If flats are more your style, forgo knitting the Mary Jane's extra strap and *viola*! You'll have a pair of flats that will make any fashionista jealous.

Sole

Rnds 1–10: Using brown, work as for the plain shoes (48 sts).

Top of Shoe

Change to the color you would like for the top of the shoe (MC).

Rnds 11–13: Knit.

Rnd 14: K23, pm, k2tog, k14, k2tog, pm, k7 (46 sts total with 16 sts between the markers).

Rnd 15: K23, sm, [k2tog] twice, sm, k7 (46 sts).

Rep Rnd 15 until there are 8 sts rem between the markers (38 sts).

Next rnd: K23, sm, join skin tone, k2tog, knit to 2 sts before marker, k2tog, sm, join MC k7.

Next rnd: K22, join skin tone, k1, sm, k2tog, knit to 2 sts before marker, k2tog, sm, k1 in skin tone, join MC, k6.

Next rnd: K21, join skin tone, k2, sm, k2tog, knit to 2 sts before marker, k2tog, sm, k2 in skin tone, join MC, k5.

Next rnd: Knit entirely in skin tone. Continue to the Legs Menu.

No Mary Jane shoe would be complete without a little strap and button. Make a strap by CO 12 sts and immediately BO. Sew over the top of the foot, and secure it with a button.

Snow Boots

When the weather gets cold, keep your doll stylishly warm with a pair of these fuzzy snow boots. They only require a color change and a separately knitted strip of "fluff" to be sewn in after they are knitted. Never before has capturing a trend been so easy.

Sole

Rnds 1–10: Using brown, work as for the plain shoes (48 sts).

Top of Boot

Change to the color you would like for the top of the boot.

Rnds 11–13: Knit.

Rnd 14: K23, pm, k2tog, k14, k2tog, pm, k7 (46 sts total, with 30 sts outside of the markers).

Rnd 15: K23, sm, k2tog, knit to 2 sts before next marker, k2tog, sm, k7 (44 sts).

Rep Rnd 15 until there are 2 sts rem between the markers (32 sts).

Next rnd: K22, [k2tog] twice (you'll have to remove the toe markers to do this), k6 (30 sts).

Knit 5 rounds.

Next rnd: To make the "fluff" for the top of the boot, join fluff yarn, knit 1 rnd and BO. You can make the top of the boot "fluffy" by rubbing the white yarn (or round) with your fingers.

When you move to the Legs Menu, CO 30 sts instead of continuing in 30 sts. Attach the snow boot by stuffing the leg into the boot, and sew them together.

Socks

Shoes aren't for everyone. Whether you are planning to knit some removable shoes later or you'd like your doll to spend her days lounging, this pair of socks is fun to knit with intarsia in the toe and color changes for stripes. Hide them under a pair of jeans or show them off with some shorts.

Rnds 1–13: Using the color of your choice (MC), work as for the plain shoes (48 sts).

Rnd 14: K23, pm, k2tog, k2, join contrasting color (CC), k10, join MC, k2, k2tog, pm, k7 (46 sts total, with 16 sts between the markers).

Rnd 15: K23, sm, k2tog, k1, join CC, k10, join MC, k1, k2tog, sm, k7 (44 sts).

Rnd 16: K23, sm, k2tog, join CC, k10, join MC, k2tog, sm, k7 (42sts).

Rnd 17: K22, join CC, k1, sm, k2tog, knit to 2 sts before marker, k2tog, sm, k1, join MC, k6 (40 sts).

Rnd 18: K21, join CC, k2, sm, k2tog, knit to 2 sts before marker, k2tog, sm, k2, join MC, k5 (38 sts).

Rnd 19: K20, join CC, k3, sm, k2tog, knit to 2 sts before marker, k2tog, sm, k3, join MC, k4 (36 sts).

Rnd 20: Knit entire round in MC.

Continue decrease until there are 2 sts rem between the markers.

Next rnd: K22, [k2tog] twice (you'll have to remove the toe markers to do this), k6 (30 sts).

Knit 2 rounds in MC, knit 1 round in CC, knit 1 round in MC, and knit last round in CC.

Make the second foot identical to the first and continue to the Legs Menu.

Flip-Flops

Let your doll show off her toes with a pair of charming flip-flops. You'll accomplish this look by knitting a separate strap and then sewing it onto your doll's feet. Complete the look by using some embroidery to add "nail polish."

Sole

Rnds 1–6: Using the color you want the bottom of the flip-flop (MC) to be, work as for plain shoes (48 sts).

Rnds 7–9: K2. Break off MC.

Top of Foot

Change to skin tone.

Rnds 10–14: Knit.

Rnd 15: K23, pm, k2tog, k14, k2tog, pm, k7 (46 sts total, with 30 sts outside of the markers).

Rep Rnd 15 until there are 2 sts rem between the markers.

Next rnd: K22, [k2tog] twice (you'll have to remove the toe markers to do this), k6 (30 sts).

Continue to the Legs Menu.

Work flip-flop strap: Using MC, CO 60 sts. Immediately BO. Sew the flip-flop "strap" onto the foot, making sure to differentiate between a left and right foot.

Make the second foot identical to the first.

How to Tie Your Shoes

What pair of sneakers can be complete without a set of laces tying them up? Of course, your knitted shoes don't need to be tied to keep them from falling off, but a creative bit of embroidery will make everyone think they do!

Cut a length of yarn about 8 inches long with whatever color you want for laces (a high contrast color to that of your main shoe color will work best). Thread each end of the yarn into its own tapestry needle and secure with a knot. Now work as though you're lacing a pair of shoes: Insert each needle into the "toe" of the shoe, about 4 stitches apart and 4 rows above the "sole" of the shoe. Pull each needle through so that there is an even length of yarn on both sides. Cross the needles, and insert them on the opposite sides of the original insertion points, one row above the previous "eyelets." Continue until you have reached the top of the shoe. Tie a bow and cut the excess yarn.

Legs Menu

You've just finished a pair of feet and the first piece of your doll. Congrats! Now that you've got a couple of shoes kicking around, you need to knit the legs to go with them. Although this part probably won't be as fun or creative as the shoes were, don't worry. After you complete this short "baby step," you'll be ready to move to the next part—pants!

Legs for Pants and Jeans

Whether you are making jeans, pants, or khakis, you will first need to make some legs for your doll. You will continue knitting in skin tone from the foot pattern of your choice with a quick color change at the end. After you're done, move on to the Pants, Shorts, and Skirts Menu.

❶ Continue knitting in skin tone for 12 rounds.

❷ Join the color for the jeans and knit 1 round.

❸ BO, leaving a 6-inch tail.

❹ Continue to the pants and jeans pattern on page 30.

Legs for Shorts

If you want to dress up your doll in a pair of shorts, you need to make the legs first. There are two different versions for you—either legs for short shorts or legs for longer "board" shorts—but both are great ways to get your doll ready for some sun.

1. Continue knitting in skin tone:

   12 rounds for **long shorts**

   20 rounds for **short shorts**

2. Break off yarn. Join color for shorts and knit 1 round.

3. BO, leaving a 6-inch tail.

4. Continue to the shorts pattern on page 33.

Tights

Giving your doll a skirt but want to keep her legs warm? How about a pair of tights? After making your two feet, you'll do a quick color change and continue knitting a full pair of legs for your doll. Finish with a skirt or an extra-long sweater.

1. Continue knitting in skin tone for 7 rounds. Break off yarn.
2. Join color for tights and knit 24 rounds. Keep the first leg on needles and continue with the second leg using a new set.
3. Knit the second leg identical to the first.
4. Join the legs and work the crotch (see the Join the Legs section on page 4 in the Basic Doll Pattern for instructions).
5. Still working in tights color, knit 10 rounds.

Underwear

Knitting a skirt for your doll? Make sure you knit her some undies. This pattern continues from the shoe of your choice and makes a full pair of legs, completed by a color change for some "boy short" style underwear. Finish up the look with the skirt of your choice.

1 Knit 30 rounds in skin tone.

2 Join the color for the underwear and knit 1 round. Keep the first leg on needles and continue the second leg using a new set.

3 Knit the second leg identical to the first.

4 Join the legs and work the crotch (see the Join the Legs section on page 4 in the Basic Doll Pattern for instructions).

5 Still working in underwear color, knit 10 rounds.

6 Continue on to one of the skirt patterns on page 34.

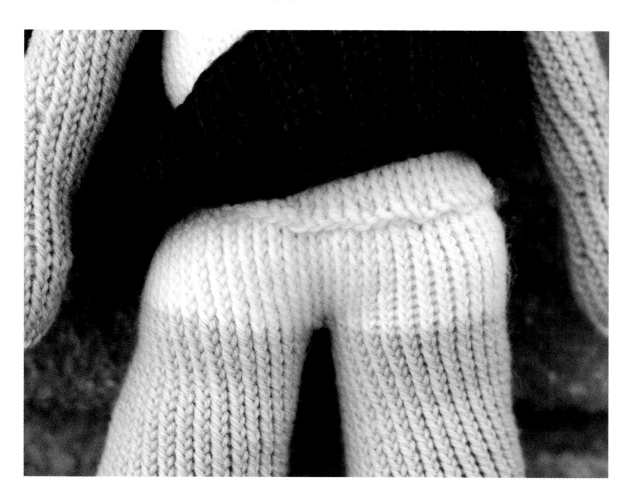

Pants, Shorts, and Skirts Menu

The old saying goes that everyone puts on their pants one leg at a time. Now that you've got legs and feet made, you can get started on knitting your doll a pair of pants (of course, one leg at a time). If pants aren't your thing, there are two different skirt patterns with three length variations, shorts, and fun little extras such as adding holes over the knees of your jeans!

Pants and Jeans

Are they called pants, trousers, or slacks? Whatever you call them, this pattern will make them all. Choose a solid color for simple slacks or khakis or pick a dark-blue heather to make some denim jeans. Add some character with cuffs or a hole over the knee!

Set-up rnd: CO 36 sts in pants color, dividing evenly onto three dpns. (For jeans, you will need to pick a denim-colored yarn. For pants, any color yarn will work.) Place marker and join in the round.

Rnds 1–10: Knit.

Rnd 11: K5, k2tog, [k10, k2tog] twice, k5 (33 sts).

Rnds 12–18: Knit.

Rnd 19: K5, k2tog, [k9, k2tog] twice, k4 (30 sts).

Rnds 20 and 21: Knit.

Sew body leg you have made to the pant leg. You do this by placing the top of the body leg inside the pant leg. Using the tail yarn of this leg, attach it to the pant leg by sewing the tail yarn into the pants. You should be attaching the leg at Rnd 20, or when the

pants are at 30 sts. When the doll has been completely stuffed, the place where the pants join the legs will function as the doll's "knees."

Rnds 22–37: Knit.

Cut the yarn, leaving a long tail. Set the first leg and stitches aside, and use a new set of needles to start the second pant leg.

Make the second pant leg.

Join the legs and work the crotch (see the Join the Legs section on page 4 in the Basic Doll Pattern for instructions).

Knit 10 more rounds.

Depending on which torso you pick for your doll, you will either join a new color and continue knitting all sts or BO all sts for the pants and CO 60 sts for the torso. Consult the pattern in the Torso Menu on page 36 to find out how to finish the pants.

Cuffs

Some people say it's tacky, but everyone's bought jeans that are too long and cuffed them up. Including cuffs with your pants pattern is a trouble-free way to add some personality to your doll—just knit a few extra rows and roll up the bottom.

Follow the pants and jeans pattern on the previous page. After the set-up round, knit 20 rounds instead of 10. Continue in the pattern. After you have attached the feet and finished the legs, fold the cuff up and sew it into place.

Holes in Jeans

Are those jeans so old that they are falling apart or are they a pair of smartly worn-out denims? You can accomplish either look with a simple bind-off, à la buttonhole. Spice it up with some embroidery around the edges for an extra-frayed look.

Follow the pants and jeans pattern through until Rnd 20.

Rnd 21: K11, BO the center 8 sts, k11.

Rnd 22: K11, CO 8 sts over the 8 sts you just BO using backward loop, k11.

Continue the jeans from Rnd 23 of the pants and jeans pattern.

Shorts

Get your doll ready for fun in the sun with a pair of shorts! This pattern includes two variations—for "short shorts" or longer "board" shorts. Both are a snap to make and knit up quickly, so you won't miss another moment of summer.

Set-up rnd: CO 32 sts in shorts color, dividing evenly onto three needles. Place a marker and join in the round.

- **For longer shorts,** knit 18 rounds.
- **For short shorts,** knit 10 rounds.

Sew the legs you have made onto the shorts. You do this by placing the top of the leg inside the bottom of the shorts. Using the tail yarn of this leg, attach it to the shorts by sewing the tail yarn into the pants. You should be attaching the leg just above the first row of your shorts.

Make the second half of the shorts for the other leg.

Join the legs and work the crotch (see the Join the Legs section on page 4 in the Basic Doll Pattern for instructions).

Knit 10 more rounds.

Depending on which torso you pick for your doll, you will either join a new color and continue knitting all sts or BO all sts for the shorts and CO 60 sts for the torso. See the Torso Menu on page 36.

Skirts

Pleated Skirt

A simple knit-two, purl-two ribbing achieves the look of this adorable pleated skirt pattern. It comes in three different lengths—short, tea, and ankle—so you can make any kind of fashion statement you want.

Set-up rnd: CO 80 sts in the color you want for your skirt, dividing evenly on three dpns. Place a marker and join in the round.

Rnd 1: *K2, p2; rep from * to end.

Rep Rnd 1:

- For a short skirt, 10 times.
- For a tea-length skirt, 20 times.
- For a long skirt, 30 times.

Next rnd: *K2, k2tog; rep from * to end (60 sts).

Knit 5 rounds, then BO, leaving a long tail.

Sew this skirt onto the doll by placing the legs you have already made inside the skirt. Using the tail yarn of the skirt, sew the skirt around the top of the joined legs, attaching it to the doll. For a removable skirt, do not sew the skirt onto the doll.

Plain Skirts

Need a simple garment for your doll? This easy skirt pattern knits up lightning quick and gives your doll an instant chic appeal. There are three different variations—for mini, tea, and ankle (or long) length skirts—so you can give your doll any look you desire.

Set-up rnd: CO 64 sts in color you want for your skirt, dividing evenly on three dpns. Place a marker and join in the round.

Rnd 1: Knit.

Rep Rnd 1:

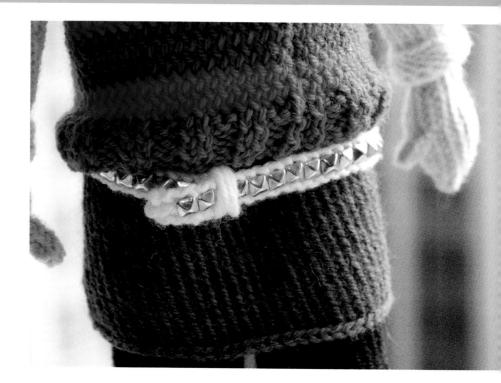

- For a mini skirt, 10 times.
- For a tea-length skirt, 20 times.
- For a long skirt, 30 times.

Next rnd: K14, k2tog, k32, k2tog, k14 (62 sts).

Knit 5 rounds, then BO.

Sew this skirt onto the doll by placing the legs you have already made inside the skirt. Using the tail yarn of the skirt, sew the skirt around the top of the joined legs, attaching it to the doll. For a removable skirt, do not sew the skirt onto the doll.

Spice up your doll's skirt with a little embroidery; try adding some lazy daisies or make any embellishments you want.

Torso Menu

Do you know that you are already half-way done with your doll? Exciting, isn't it? Now that you're in the home stretch, it's time to get *really* creative. With everything from intarsia shirt designs and colorful stripes to bold letters and numbers for jerseys, you can never run out of ideas for what kind of top you will put on your doll's back.

Angelica

Head with hair template, p. 54
Long hair, p. 56
Hand with fingers, p. 71
Arms for long sleeves, p. 74
Turtleneck, p. 42
Angel wings, p. 91
Pants, p. 30
Snow boots, p. 18

If you would like to create a more realistic-looking sweater or T-shirt, bind off the 60 stitches from the legs or pants, and cast on 60 stitches at the beginning of any option from the Torso Menu. Sew the torso over the legs and *voila!* It will look like the shirt is lying over the pants.

T-Shirt

The T-shirt is such an adaptable garment in today's world that it is hard to think it has only been worn as a fashionable top since the 1950s. Although this pattern just gives you the basics for knitting a T-shirt, don't let the empty stitches get you down. Check out the Repeating Designs section for ways to enhance your doll's T-shirt, or use a blank chart in the Appendix to design a shirt that is all your own.

Join color for T-shirt.

Rnds 1–15: Knit.

Rnd 16: *K8, k2tog; rep from * to end (54 sts).

Rnds 17–25: Knit.

Rnd 26: *K7, k2tog; rep from * to end (48 sts).

Rnds 27–30: Knit.

Rnd 31: *K4, k2tog; rep from * to end (40 sts).

Rnd 32: Knit.

Join skin color.

Rnds 33 and 34: Knit.

Rnd 35 (shape neck): *K2, k2tog; rep from * to end (30 sts).

Rnds 36–38: Knit.

Rnd 39: *K2, m1; rep from * to end (45 sts).

Rnd 40: Knit.

Rnd 41: *K3, m1; rep from * to end (60 sts).

From here, go to the Head and Face Menu on page 52.

Ringer T-shirt Variation: A simple variation of the T-shirt is the *ringer*, which has bands of ribbing on the sleeves and collar in a contrasting color. All you'll need to do is a quick color change along the neckline in a darker-hued yarn during Round 32 of the T-shirt. When you are knitting the sleeves of your T-shirt, knit the first row of the short sleeve in the same contrasting color. Consider the same personalizing suggestions as the T-shirt pattern, such as adding designs or stripes.

Halter Top Variation: A sexy way to keep cool in the summer, the halter top is a breeze to knit for your doll. All you need to do to create this look is a color change halfway through the torso pattern. To create a halter top, knit the first 26 rounds of the torso in the shirt color of your choice. Switch to the skin tone and finish the torso. It's that easy! Consider putting some blush on your doll's shoulders to give her a sun-kissed look.

V-Neck Sweater

Sweaters are one of those iconic knitting projects that every knitter has attempted at least once. Now you can try it in miniature. These sweaters have classic ribbing along the sleeves, neck, and bottom, and come in three different variations—turtleneck, crew neck, and V-neck. You can easily give your doll a perfectly delightful sweater. Spice up your sweater by using the same Nordic flower design that is used on the Swedish Ski Cap (see page 111).

Join the color for the V-neck sweater.

Rnds 1–5: *K2, p2; rep from * to end.

Rnds 6–15: Knit.

Rnd 16: *K8, k2tog; rep from * to end (54 sts).

Rnds 17–25: Knit.

Rnd 26: *K7, k2tog; rep from * to end (48 sts).

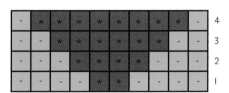

* Skin tone

- Sweater color

Rnds 27–30: K24, work next 10 sts following the V-neck chart in a skin tone, knit rem 14 sts in sweater color. Follow the chart for the next 3 rounds. You can also use a color for an "undershirt" for this part if you'd like.

Rnd 31: *K4, k2tog; rep from * to end (40 sts).

Rnd 32: Knit.

Join skin tone color.

Rnds 33 and 34: Knit.

Rnd 35 (shape neck): *K2, k2tog; rep from * to end (30 sts).

Rnds 36–38: Knit.

Rnd 39: *K2, m1; rep from * to end (45 sts).

Rnd 40: Knit.

Rnd 41: *K3, m1; rep from * to end (60 sts).

Continue to the Head and Face Menu starting on page 52.

V-Neck Ribbing

CO 50 sts in color for V-neck sweater.

Rows 1–3: *K2, p2; rep from * to end. This is worked flat.

BO in rib pattern.

Sew around the neck of the doll, following the skin tone or undershirt pattern to create the appearance of a V-neck sweater.

Turtleneck Sweater

Start the turtleneck by following the V-neck sweater pattern on page 40 through Rnd 31 (40 sts).

Rnds 32–41: *K2, p2; rep from * to end.

BO in rib pattern, leaving a 6-inch tail. Set the sweater aside while you work the neck and head.

Neck and Head

CO 40 sts in skin tone.

Rnds 1 and 2: Knit.

Rnd 3 (shape neck): *K2, k2tog; rep from * to end (30 sts).

Rnds 4–6: Knit.

Rnd 7: *K2, m1; rep from * to end (45 sts).

Rnd 8: Knit.

Rnd 9: *K3, m1; rep from * to end (60 sts).

From here, continue to the Head and Face Menu starting on page 52.

After completing the head, sew the neck onto the sweater, along Rnd 31, the last round of the sweater before the ribbing for the turtle neck. Fold the ribbing of the turtleneck in half, inward, and weave in all the ends.

Crew Neck Sweater Variation: For a crew neck sweater, follow the pattern for the turtleneck sweater, but make only Rounds 32–34 (3 rounds) of 2 × 2 ribbing for the neck. Continue with the neck and head.

Longer Sweater Variation: For a longer sweater, start by knitting 10 rounds of 2 × 2 ribbing instead of 5 rounds. Continue to the sweater pattern of your choice.

Stripes

What better way to add worry-free color to your doll than with these distinctive striping templates? With everything from classic rugby stripes to stripes of alternating thicknesses, all you'll need to do to brighten up your project is to pick out your favorite colors.

Stripes are fun, easy, and add loads of color to your doll. Since the torso won't use up quite so much yarn, you can always use scraps from other projects. It's a great way to use up any stash you have laying around. You can use any repeating stripe patterns you want.

^	^	^	^	^	10
^	^	^	^	^	9
-	-	-	-	-	8
^	^	^	^	^	7
^	^	^	^	^	6
*	*	*	*	*	5
*	*	*	*	*	4
+	+	+	+	+	3
*	*	*	*	*	2
*	*	*	*	*	1

^	Color 1
-	Color 2
*	Color 3
+	Color 4

^	^	^	^	^	10
^	^	^	^	^	9
^	^	^	^	^	8
^	^	^	^	^	7
^	^	^	^	^	6
*	*	*	*	*	5
*	*	*	*	*	4
*	*	*	*	*	3
*	*	*	*	*	2
*	*	*	*	*	1

| * | Color 1 |
| ^ | Color 2 |

To create the stripes shown in the photo on the previous page, you will repeat the stripe pattern 3½ times since the torso is 35 rows long. This means that you will start and finish with Colors 1 and 2.

To create the rugby stripes seen in the photo on the left, you will repeat the stripe pattern 3½ times since the torso is 35 rows long, meaning that you will start and finish with Color 1.

When you have finished working in stripes, continue by going to Rnd 33 in the T-shirt pattern (page 38) or sweater pattern (page 40).

A Word about Vertical Stripes

Vertical stripes are something you may want to stay away from, and here's why: Because of the decreasing rows, your vertical stripes will end up becoming skinnier and skinner. Also, if you have a lot of tension when you knit, your stripes will curve slightly and won't be perfectly vertical. You're obviously free to try out some vertical stripes for yourself, but keep this in mind.

Repeating Designs

Repeating designs have always been a popular motif on everything from shirts to skirts. As long as you keep in mind the decreasing rows, you shouldn't have any problems. Violet's hearts (shown here) is a good example of a repeating pattern.

Follow the torso pattern of your choice. Violet's hearts pattern is designed so that you will decrease on the rounds between the hearts. After each decrease round, you will get one fewer heart. If you keep the start of your round as the "back" of your doll, the hearts will line up correctly on her "front."

^	^		^	^		^	^		^	^		10
^	^		^	^		^	^		^	^	^	9
^				^	^	^				^	^	8
					^						^	7
												6
*	*		*	*		*	*		*	*		5
*	*		*	*		*	*		*	*		4
	*	*	*				*	*	*			3
	*							*				2
												1

	Main Color
*	Color 1
^	Color 2

Single Designs

Don't leave your doll in a boring top. Dress up any shirt or sweater with an intarsia design (see the sidebar, "Working Instarsia in the Round?" on page 16). These can also be worked in duplicate stitch if you don't feel comfortable with working instarsia. A skull and crossbones motif is provided as well as an adorable bear logo, but feel free to use a blank chart in the Appendix to make your own design.

		*	*				*	*		9
	*	-	-	*	*	*	-	-	*	8
	*	-	*	*	*	*	*	-	*	7
		*	*	*	*	*	*	*		6
	*	*	*	*	*	*	*	*	*	5
	*	*	^	*	*	*		*	*	4
	*	*	*	-		-	*	*	*	3
		*	*	-	-	-	*	*		2
			*	*	*	*	*			1

- Main color
- * Color 1
- - Color 2
- (black) Color 3

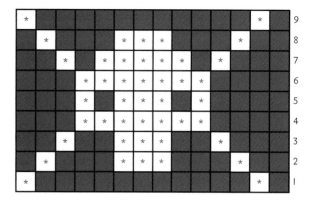

*											*		9
	*				*	*	*			*			8
		*		*	*	*	*	*		*			7
			*	*	*	*	*	*	*				6
		*		*	*	*		*					5
		*	*	*	*	*	*	*					4
	*			*	*	*			*				3
*				*	*	*			*				2
*										*			1

■ Main color

* │ Color 1

The designs are made to fit in between Rounds 17 and 25 of the torso pattern.

Alphabet

Whether it's the name of your favorite band or the acronym for your university, you can give your doll a shirt that says anything. By using the handy alphabet pattern and a blank chart that is provided in the Appendix, you can plot out your message and make certain you have enough space to fit all your letters on the front of your doll's shirt.

47

Numbers

Numbers can say so much more than their numerical value. Ask a pro athlete why he chose the number he wears, and it could be the year he was born, the age he was at when something really significant happened in his life or just his lucky number. With the numbers chart and a blank chart in the Appendix, you can knit your own secret message for your doll and say something about yourself in a truly unique way.

Hockey Sweater

Before polyester jerseys, hockey uniforms were knitted wool sweaters with the team name woven across the front. Knit your doll supporting the team that you follow or make a cuddly version of your favorite player. Use a blank chart in the Appendix to put a number on the back and perhaps add a captain's "C" on the front. Replicate an authentic sweater by purchasing a 2-inch × 2-inch embroidered patch from your team and sewing it to your doll's chest.

Note: The hockey sweater is longer than the other torso patterns because it is intended to lie over the pants. You will have to bind off the 60 stitches of your doll's pants and cast on 60 stitches to start the hockey sweater. When you have finished knitting the torso, sew it onto the doll's pants by stuffing the pants into the torso and sewing along Rnd 4.

CO 60 sts in Color 3. Divide evenly onto three dpns, pm, and join in the round.

Rnds 1–4: Knit.

Rnd 5: Switch to black, knit.

Switch to primary team Color 2.

Rnds 6–9: Knit.

Switch to black.

Rnd 10: Knit.

Switch to Color 3.

Rnds 11–13: Knit.

Switch to primary team Color 1.

Rnds 14–18: Knit.

Rnd 19: *K8, k2tog; rep from * to end (54 sts).

Rnds 20–29: If you would like to add a player number, do so now on the back of the jersey by using a blank chart in the Appendix and the numbers chart on page 131. Use Color 3 or white for the numbers.

Rnd 30: *K7, k2tog; rep from * to end (48 sts).

Rnds 31–33: Knit.

Rnd 34: *K4, k2tog; rep from * to end (40 sts).

Rnd 35: Knit.

BO.

Continue by using the turtleneck sweater's neck and head pattern on page 42. Then make the hockey sweater sleeves using the instructions on page 81.

If you included a player number, thread a needle with about 6 inches of Color 3 or white yarn. Using a back stitch, embroider on your player number (as shown on the previous page) over Rnds 30–35 in the sleeve.

Polo Shirt

The Polo shirt could be a stylishly laid-back top to wear everyday or a casually sophisticated shirt for work. You will start by knitting in the round, and then switch to knitting flat for the collar. Follow the chart provided to give your doll a lovable checkered shirt, or make up your own design. Finish by sewing on a few buttons.

Note: The Polo shirt pattern is written to include a "Gingham" style design chart. This chart includes vertical stripes, which means that if you have a high amount of tension, the vertical stripes may start to curve. Use your best judgment before choosing to work in this chart.

Join the color for the Polo shirt main color (MC).

Rnd 1: Knit.

Join Colors 1 and 2.

Rnds 2–15: Knit, following Gingham design chart.

Rnd 16: *K8, k2tog; rep from * to end (54 sts).

Note: Because you will be decreasing sts, every other "box" of the Gingham design will be reduced by 1 stitch during this row. Continue the Gingham design as though you had not decreased. In other words,

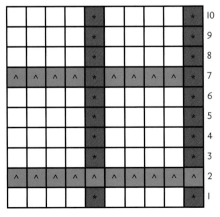

Legend	
(white)	Main color
*	Color 1
^	Color 2

continue working the vertical stripes where they are on the torso—do not move them to accommodate the pattern.

Rnds 17–25: Knit.

Rnd 26: *K7, k2tog; rep from * to end (48 sts).

Rnds 27–30: Knit.

Rnd 31: Cut off Colors 1 and 2, leaving tails to weave in later. Work from here in the main color only. Knit.

Rnd 32: *K4, k2tog; rep from * to end (40 sts).

Rnd 33 (begin working collar): Knit to end of row, turn, and begin working flat.

Row 1: Purl.

Rows 2–5: Rep last row four more times.

BO. When you lay the collar flat, the purl side of the St st will show.

Continue by using the turtleneck sweater's neck and head pattern on page 42.

Head and Face Menu

Now it's time to knit your doll a face and give her (or him) a personality! Welcome to the Head and Face Menu. Here you can use a template to add hair, maybe embroider a nose, use techniques to create any hairstyle you want, or even add stubble or freckles. Make sure that you have a pair of plastic eyes at the ready.

Head with Hair Template

If you are planning to give your doll a head full of hair, you need to start here. Using this template will create a setting for your doll's hair by joining new yarn in the same color as the hair you will use, which will give you a more realistic head once you've threaded in the hair. Move to the Hairstyles section after you are done to find inspiration from choices on how to finish your doll.

If you would like a head without hair, consult the Head and Face section in the Basic Doll Pattern. Use this pattern if you are going to be sewing in hair later on. Also see the sidebar "Working Intarsia in the Round?" on page 16.

Continue from where you left off on the torso with 60 sts.

Rnd 1: Knit.

Rnd 2: Join color for hair, k15; k30 in skin color for face; return to hair color and knit rem 15 sts.

Rnds 3–13: Working in color pattern just established, knit.

Rnd 14: K16 in hair color; k28 in skin color for face; k16 in hair color.

Rnd 15: K17 in hair color; k26 in skin color for face; k17 in hair color.

Rnd 16: K18 in hair color; k24 in skin color; k18 in hair color.

Rnd 17: *K4, k2tog, pm; rep from * to end (50 sts).

Rnd 18: Knit entirely with the hair color, without decreasing.

Before continuing with head shaping, stuff the body and head. Place the eyes, following the instructions in the Basic Doll Pattern on page 7.

Rnd 19: *Knit to 2 sts before marker, k2tog, sm; rep from * to end (40 sts).

Rnd 20: Knit.

Rnd 21: *K2, k2tog; rep from * to end (30 sts).

Rnd 22: Knit.

Rnd 23: *K1, k2tog; rep from * to end (20 sts).

Rnd 24: Knit.

Rnd 25: *K2tog; rep from * to end (10 sts).

Break off the yarn, thread through rem sts, and pull it tight. Continue to Hairstyles section.

Hairstyles

Now that you've finished your doll's head using the hair template, you need to learn how to give your doll a hairstyle. This section includes everything you will need to know to create a smorgasbord of hairstyles—ranging from long to swoopy bangs to Mohawks. You'll need a crochet hook, scissors, and a lot of yarn to achieve the most realistic hair for your doll.

Below and on the following pages are listed a few starting ideas for how to give your doll different hairstyles. Each point in the illustrations represents where you should insert a strand of hair. For short hairstyles, you will have to add hair evenly over the surface of the head. Of course these are only examples, and you can make up your own hairstyles as well—the length of your doll's hair is up to you.

Highlights Variation: If you want to give your doll highlights, add a few lighter toned pieces of yarn.

Use the following illustrations to determine where you will need to add hair for **bangs**, a **ponytail**, or a **Mohawk**.

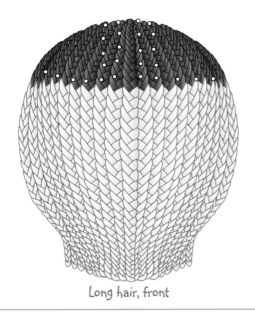

Long hair, front

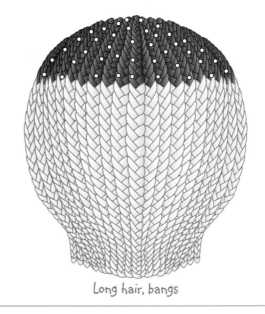

Long hair, bangs

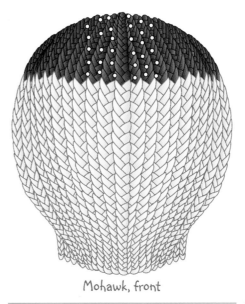

Mohawk, front

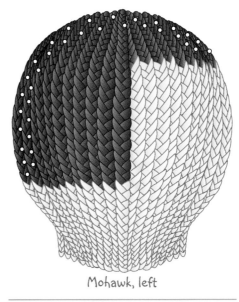

Mohawk, left

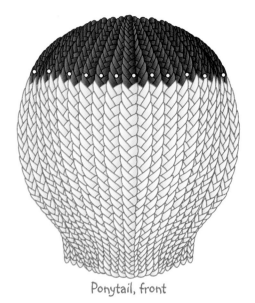

Ponytail, front

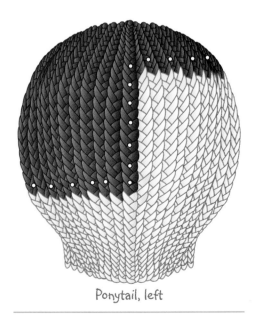

Ponytail, left

To tie up hair in ponytails or pigtails, you can secure the "tails" with a piece of yarn in a different color. You should not use rubber bands, as they can degrade over time and can ruin the yarn in the doll's hair.

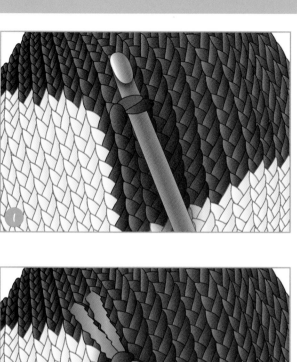

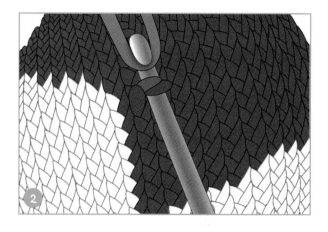

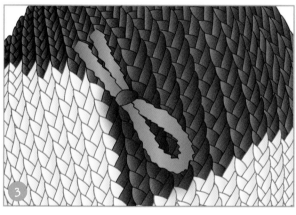

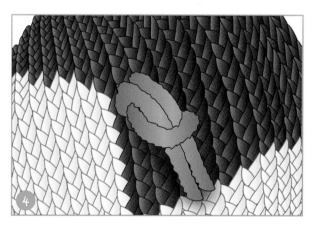

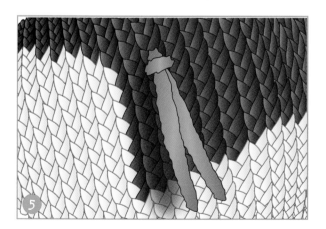

To apply the hair, you will insert your crochet hook into the top of the doll's head (1). Take your hair yarn and fold it in half. Catch the fold in the crochet hook (2) and pull it through the doll's head (3). Secure it by pulling the ends through the loop (4 and 5).

Nose

Protruding Nose

For some odd reason, most knitted dolls don't ever seem to come with a nose and yet, sometimes the most distinguishing part of a person is a really distinctive shnoz. So if you simply have to add a nose to give your doll a unique personality, you're in luck! Instead of buying a plastic nose as shown in the photo, use this pattern. It is a variant of the normal head pattern that includes a series of decreases in the head itself to create a protruding nose, which is great to use for animal dolls.

Continue from where you left off on the torso with 60 sts.

Rnd 1: Knit.

Rnd 2: *K6, m1; rep from * to end (70 sts).

Rnd 3: K29, pm, k2tog, k8, k2tog, pm, knit to end (68 sts).

Rnd 4: Knit to first marker, sm, k2tog, knit to 2 sts before second marker, k2tog, sm, knit to end (66 sts).

Rnds 5–7: Rep last round three more times, until 60 sts rem. Remove markers.

Rnds 8–16: Knit.

Rnd 17: *K4, k2tog, pm; rep from * to end (50 sts).

Rnd 18: Knit.

Before continuing with the head shaping, stuff the body and head. Place the eyes, following the instructions in the Basic Doll Pattern on page 7.

Rnd 19: *Knit to 2 sts before marker, k2tog, sm; rep from * to end (40 sts).

Rnd 20: Knit.

Rnd 21: *K2, k2tog; rep from * to end (30 sts).

Rnd 22: Knit.

Rnd 23: *K1, k2tog; rep from * to end (20 sts).

Rnd 24: Knit.

Rnd 25: *K2tog; rep from * to end (10 sts).

Break off the yarn, thread through rem sts, and pull it tight.

Expressions

Whether you want your doll to be pouting or smiling, she won't be complete until she has an expression on her face. This is a snap to do with a bit of embroidery. Below are instructions for two basic facial expressions, but you can use your imagination and create any kind of expression you want.

After you have stuffed the head and added the eyes, thread a needle with about 10 inches of black yarn or embroidery floss.

For a basic smile: The starting point for your doll's smile should be somewhere evenly spaced between the two eyes and about three rows below the eyes. Using the back stitch, create a straight line over the three center stitches of the face. Next, create the points of the smile by adding a line about one stitch away and one stitch up from the center line, on both sides of the line. (See Rusty in first photo.)

For a pout: The starting point for your doll's smile should be somewhere evenly spaced between the two eyes and about three rows below the eyes. From the starting point, use the back stitch to create a line at a downward diagonal, going about two rows and three stitches away from the starting point, on either side of the starting point. (See Violet in second photo.)

Facial Hair

Not every doll should look adorable—some need to have an edge to them. Perhaps you know someone with a hip soul patch you'd like to knit? Or maybe you want to create a hockey player working on that play-off beard? It's easy to make your doll tough by adding some facial hair. All you have to do is either change a color or add some duplicate stitch to give your doll the attitude he needs.

Stubble

After you have stuffed the head and added the eyes, thread a needle with about 10 inches of yarn in the hair color. Using a duplicate stitch, add stubble where you desire.

Soul Patch

After you have stuffed the head and added the eyes, thread a needle with about 10 inches of yarn in the hair color. Using a satin stitch, create a soul patch under the doll's mouth.

Freckles

Beautiful and endearing, freckles can add tons of personality to your doll and are truly easy to create. All you need to do is add a few duplicate stitches to your doll's face after you're done placing the eyes and stuffing. You can also use this technique to add beauty marks, à la Marilyn Monroe!

After you have stuffed the head and added the eyes, thread a needle with about 10 inches of yarn in a light red or brown. Using either the duplicate stitch or French knots, add about three to five freckles under each eye. You can add more if desired.

Makeup

To add some extra life and color to your doll, why not try using some makeup? You can use a pale shade of blush to gently brush onto cheeks, elbows, shoulders, knees or anywhere a little color is needed. You can also add eye shadow above the eyes. Use only powder makeup that won't get too imbedded into the fabric. Use a brand of blush that will easily wash off with cold water. Don't apply the makeup too roughly or it will be more difficult to remove. You also run the risk of accidentally felting the doll if you apply it too roughly.

Fangs

Are you knitting a pug with an adorable underbite? Or maybe a sexy vampire ready to bite? Either way, your doll is going to need some teeth. Fangs are an incredibly easy addition to your doll. All you need to do is a little bit of duplicate stitching under (or over) the ends of your doll's smile. But don't worry—even with some teeth, your doll will always be ready to cuddle.

After you have stuffed the head and added the eyes, thread a needle with about 6 inches of white yarn. Using a duplicate stitch, add a "fang" underneath each end of your doll's facial expression.

Hand and Arm Menu

Way to go! You've made it this far and now you are only one step away from completing your own doll. Here you will find patterns for knitting hands and arms. This menu is broken up into three stages for knitting an arm—including the hand and sleeve choices. If you want a doll with a touch more realism, try the mitten-like thumb pattern, or be really ambitious and attempt the fingers pattern. Prepare yourself for a completed journey and a cuddly new friend.

Becky

Hand with Thumb

Want to make your knitted doll look a little bit more like a bona fide human? Thumbs are the way to go. You'll start by knitting a separate I-cord "thumb," which you will later join to the rest of the hand. Knit from the fingertips to the wrist, the hand-with-thumb pattern is worked like a mitten in reverse. Although it's a bit challenging, the payoff is well worth it!

Thumb

CO 6 sts. Divide evenly onto two needles, join to begin knitting in the round.

Rnds 1–3: Knit.

Rnd 4: BO first 2 sts, knit to end of round (4 sts). Move all sts to one needle and set aside.

Hand

CO 10 sts, leaving a 2-inch tail.

Divide evenly onto three dpns, pm, and join to begin knitting in round.

Rnd 1: Knit.

Rnd 2: *K2, m1; rep from * to end of round (15 sts).

Rnds 3–7: Knit.

Rnd 8: For left hand: BO *first* 3 sts, then knit to end of round. **For right hand:** Knit to *last* 3 sts of round and BO 3 (12 sts).

Rnd 9 (joining the thumb): For left hand: Move 4 thumb sts onto first of the three dpns so they begin the round, matching up the 2 bound-off thumb sts with the 3 bound-off hand sts. **For right hand:** Move 4 thumb sts onto last of the three dpns so they end the round, matching up the 2 bound-off thumb sts with the 3 bound-off hand sts. Knit both hand and thumb sts together, making 16 total hand sts.

Rnds 10–15: Knit.

Rnd 16: *K2, k2tog; rep from * to end of round (12 sts).

Keep the hand stitches on the needles and set them aside. Using a new set of needles, make the second hand—if you knitted a left hand, knit a right hand, and vice versa. Sew together the bottom of the hand and sew closed the join between the thumb and the hand. Continue to the arm of your choice.

Hand with Fingers

If you are feeling very adventurous, give the fingers pattern a try. You'll begin by knitting four separate I-cord "fingers," join them all together to form a palm, and then add an I-cord "thumb." Although this may be one of the more difficult patterns in this book, you'll be rewarded by an impressive-looking and eye-catching hand!

Thumb

CO 6 sts. Divide evenly onto two needles, and join in the round.

Rnds 1–3: Knit.

Rnd 4: BO first 2 sts, knit to end of round (4 sts). Move all sts to one needle and set aside.

Pinky Finger

CO 4 sts. Divide evenly onto two needles, and join to begin knitting in the round.

Rnds 1–4: Knit.

Set aside by placing on two spare needles, 2 sts on each needle.

Ring Finger

CO 4 sts. Divide evenly onto two needles, and join to begin knitting in the round.

Rnds 1–4: Knit.

Put stitches aside on the two spare needles you placed the pinky finger on, 2 sts on each needle.

Middle Finger

CO 4 sts. Divide evenly onto two needles, and join to begin knitting in the round.

Rnds 1–5: Knit.

Set aside by placing on the two spare needles, following the ring and pinky fingers, 2 sts on each needle.

Index Finger

CO 4 sts. Divide evenly onto two needles, and join to begin knitting in the round.

Rnds 1–4: Knit.

Set aside by placing on the two spare needles, following the middle, ring, and pinky fingers, 2 sts on each needle. From left to right, you will have the pinky finger, followed by the ring, middle, and index fingers.

Hand

Joining the fingers: The fingers are now on two needles, from left to right—pinky, ring, middle, and index. Both needles have 2 sts from each finger—one needle has 2 pinky sts, 2 ring sts, 2 middle sts, and 2 index sts (making 8 total sts on each needle) and the other needle has the same. Remember that the placement of the fingers on the needles is the same for both right and left hands.

Set-up rnd: Move the finger sts from two needles to three dpns by dividing the sts of one needle evenly onto two needles—the first dpn has 2 pinky sts, 2 ring sts, 2 middle sts, and 2 index sts. The second dpn has 2 pinky sts and 2 ring sts, and the third dpn has 2 middle sts and 2 index sts.

Knit all finger stitches in order on three dpns, making 16 hand sts altogether. Place marker, and join in the round.

Rnds 1–5: Knit.

Rnd 6: For left hand, BO first 4 sts then knit to end of round (these 4 sts are over the index and middle fingers). **For right hand,** knit to last 4 sts of round, BO 4 (these 4 sts are over the middle and index fingers)—12 sts.

Rnd 7 (joining the thumb): For left hand: Move 4 thumb sts onto first of the three dpns so they begin the round, matching up the 2 bound-off thumb sts with the 3 bound-off hand sts. **For right hand:** Move 4 thumb sts onto last of the three dpns so they end the round, matching up the 2 bound-off thumb sts with the 3 bound-off hand sts. Knit both hand and thumb sts together, making 16 total hand sts.

Rnds 8–12: Knit.

Rnd 13: *K2, k2tog; rep from * to end of round (12 sts).

Keep the hand stitches on the needles and set aside. Using a new set of needles, make the second hand—if you knitted a left hand, knit a right hand, and vice versa. Sew together the bottom of the hand and sew closed the join between the thumb and hand. Continue to the arm of your choice.

Arms

Now that you've got your hands knitted, it's time to move to the arms. Just like the legs you've already made, you will need to knit the arms of your doll as a precursor to knitting the sleeves. And just like the legs, you've got a few options: You can make your arms fitted for either short sleeves or long sleeves. After you're finished, move to the sleeve of your choice.

Arms for Short Sleeves

If you want to give your doll some short sleeves, start knitting here. You'll simply continue knitting from the hand and finish with an easy bind-off. From there, continue on to the short sleeve pattern.

Continue from the hand pattern of your choice.

Rnds 1–5: Knit.

Rnd 6: K3, m1, k6, m1, k3 (14 sts).

Rnds 7–16: Knit.

Rnd 17: K4, m1, k6, m1, k4 (16 sts).

Rnds 18–32: Knit.

Rnd 33: BO.

From here, continue to the short sleeve pattern on page 76.

Arms for Long Sleeves

Want a doll wearing a sweater or long sleeved T-shirt? Then this is the pattern for you. Continue knitting from your doll's hands and finish with a bind-off before continuing on to the long sleeves pattern of your choice.

Continue from the hand pattern of your choice.

Rnds 1–5: Knit.

Rnd 6: K3, m1, k6, m1, k3 (14 sts).

Rnds 7–16: Knit.

Rnd 17: Switch to main color (MC) of the sleeve and knit 1 round.

Rnd 18: BO and leave a 6-inch long tail.

From here, continue to the long sleeves pattern on page 78.

Sleeves

Short Sleeves

You have nearly finished your doll's arms. If you're knitting your doll in a T-shirt, these are the sleeves you will need to knit. They are knit flat in a stockinette stitch, and then sewn around the top of the arm you've already made. Once you've finished your doll's torso, you'll sew the entire arm on to your doll.

CO 16 sts in the color of the shirt.

Rows 1 and 2: Knit.

Row 3: *K2tog, knit to last 2 sts of row, k2tog (14 sts).

Row 4 (WS): Purl.*

Rep from * to * until there are 8 sts. Remember, if your doll's torso has a design, take care to maintain it while decreasing in the short sleeve. BO, leaving a long tail.

Sew the arm to the short sleeve by wrapping the short sleeve around the top of the arm, at Rnd 32 of the arm. Using the tail from the short sleeve, sew the sleeve onto the arm so that the sleeve lies on top of the arm. Stuff the arms.

Make the second sleeve like the first.

Sew the arms with attached sleeves onto the doll's body. Consult the Basic Doll Pattern on page 9 for instructions.

Puffed Short Sleeves

Similar to the short sleeves, puffed sleeves are knitted flat without any decreasing. Once you're done knitting the sleeves, you will fold the top, creating some pleats and a "puffy" appearance. Once your doll's torso is done, you will knit your doll's arms to the body.

CO 16 sts in color of shirt.

Row 1: *Knit.

Row 2: Purl*.

Rep from * to * for 9 more rows.

BO. Fold the top edge of the sleeve so that it creates a pleat resulting in a "puffed" appearance.

Sew the arm to the puffed sleeve by wrapping the puffed sleeve around the top of the arm, at Rnd 32 of the arm. Using the tail from the short sleeve, sew the sleeve onto the arm so that the sleeve lies on top of the arm. Stuff the arms.

Make the second sleeve like the first.

Sew the arms with the attached sleeves onto the doll's body. See the Basic Doll Pattern on page 9 for instructions.

Long Sleeves

You've done the first two parts of making your doll's arms, and now it's time to start on the final piece—the sleeves. This pattern is for a long-sleeved T-shirt, which is initially knit in the round and then knit flat to form a realistic shoulder. Once you are done with your doll's torso, you can sew the entire arm onto your doll.

CO 16 sts, leaving a 6-inch tail.

Divide evenly onto three dpns, and join to begin knitting in the round.

Rnds 1–35: Knit.

Rnd 36: *K2tog, knit to last 2 sts, k2tog (14 sts).

Next row: Turn and purl.*

Working flat from here, rep from * to * until 8 sts rem.

BO, leaving a long tail.

Sew the arm to the long sleeve by stuffing the arm into the sleeve. Using the tail from the arm, sew the sleeve onto the arm, at Rnd 20 of the long sleeve. Stuff the arms.

Make the second sleeve like the first.

Sew the arms with the attached sleeves onto the doll's body. See the Basic Doll Pattern on page 9 for instructions.

Long-Sleeve Undershirts

Can't decide between long-sleeves and short-sleeves? Why not do both? This pattern will give you a long-sleeved "undershirt" to sew under a short sleeve. Finish by knitting a pair of short sleeves.

CO 16 sts, leaving a 2-inch tail.

Divide evenly onto three dpns, and join to begin knitting in the round.

Rnds 1–35: Knit.

BO, leaving a short tail. Make yourself a pair of short sleeves following the pattern on page 76, and sew the long-sleeve undershirt underneath the short sleeves.

Attach the short sleeve to the long-sleeved undershirt as follows: Sew the short sleeve to the undershirt by wrapping the short sleeve around the top of the undershirt, at Rnd 35. Using the tail from the short sleeve, sew the sleeve onto the undershirt, so that the sleeve lies on top of the undershirt.

Sew the arm into the long-sleeved undershirt as follows: Sew the arm into the undershirt by stuffing the arm into the undershirt. Using the tail from the arm, sew the arm into the undershirt at Rnd 20 of the undershirt. Stuff the arm.

Make the second sleeve like the first.

Sew the arms with the attached sleeves onto the doll's body. See the Basic Doll Pattern on page 9 for instructions.

Sweater Sleeves

Starting with an easy 2 × 2 ribbing, these sleeves will replicate the look of a sweater. You will start by knitting in the round, and then switch to knitting flat for realistic, sloped shoulders. Once your doll's torso is knitted, you can sew the arms onto the doll.

CO 16 sts, leaving a 6-inch tail.

Divide evenly onto three dpns, and join to begin knitting in the round.

Rnds 1–5: *K2, p2; rep from * to end.

Rnds 6–35: Knit.

Rnd 36: *K2tog, knit to last 2 sts, k2tog.

Next row: Turn and purl.*

Rep from * to * until 8 sts rem. BO.

Sew the arm to the long sleeve by stuffing the arm into the sleeve. Using the tail from the arm, sew the sleeve onto the arm at Rnd 20 of the long sleeve. Stuff the arms.

Hockey Sweater Sleeves

The following instructions are to knit the sleeves for the hockey sweater on page 48.

CO 16 sts in the primary team Color 1, leaving a 6-inch tail.

Divide evenly onto three dpns, pm, and join in the round.

Rnds 1–12: Knit.

Change to Color 3.

Rnd 13: Knit.

Change to black.

Rnd 14: Knit.

Change to team Color 2.

Rnds 15–18: Knit.

Change to black.

Rnd 19: Knit.

Change to Color 3.

Rnd 20: Knit.

Change to primary team Color 1.

Rnds 21–35: Knit.

Rnd 36: *K2tog, knit to last 2 sts, k2tog; turn and work flat (14 sts).

Next row: Purl.*

Rep from * to * until 8 sts rem.

BO.

Sew the arm sleeve onto the torso. See the Basic Doll Pattern on page 9 for instructions.

Can You Believe It?

After knitting the arms and sleeves, you have just finished making your very own doll! It was quite a journey, wasn't it? From here, you can continue to the Accessories Menu on page 102 to give your doll a few cute extras, or, you can simply celebrate the fact that your doll has finally come together.

Mythical Creatures and More Anatomical Features

Mermaids and angels? Kittens and teddy bears? It's time to get a little magical. If human dolls are a little too dull for you, try adding some of these extra anatomical features to your knits. Turn the stuff of day dreams into cuddly reality!

Milo

Mermaid

No other magical creatures have quite the appeal of a mermaid. Mysterious and beautiful creatures of the sea, mermaids (and mermen) embody playfulness and charm. This pattern replaces the doll's legs with a tail and a stunning set of mermaid's fins; it even included an optional "seashell" top. This is one knitted doll that's sure to make a splash.

Tail

CO 6 sts.

Rnd 1: Knit.

Rnd 2: *K1, m1; rep from * to end (12 sts)

Rnds 3–6: Knit.

Rnd 7: *K4, m1, pm; rep from * to end (15 sts).

Rnds 8–10: Knit.

Rnd 11: *K to marker, m1, sm; rep from * to end (18 sts).

Rnds 12–14: Knit.

Rep rnds 11–14, shaping as established, until you have 60 sts.

Next rnd (hip shaping): K7, BO 7, knit to end (53 sts). The piece will now be worked flat.

Row 1: K2tog, knit to end of row, k2tog (51 sts).

Row 2: K2tog, purl to end of row, k2tog (49 sts).

Repeat Rows 1 and 2 twice more, ending with 45 sts.

BO. Continue to the torso section of the Basic Doll Pattern on page 6. CO 60 sts (instead of continuing to work in sts) and work the torso pattern as usual. When you have completed the torso, sew the mermaid tail to the torso by stuffing the torso into the tail, making sure that the 7 BO sts in the hip shaping are centered correctly. Sew along the 5th round of the torso.

Fins

CO 4 sts, divide onto three dpns, and join to knit in the round.

Rnd 1: Knit.

Rnd 2: *K2, m1; rep from * to end (6 sts).

Rnd 3: Knit.

Rnd 4: *K1, m1; rep from * to end (12 sts).

Rnds 5 and 6: Knit.

Rnd 7: *K2, m1; rep from * to end (18 sts).

Rnds 8 and 9: Knit.

Rnd 10: *K2, m1: rep from * to end (27 sts).

Rnds 11 and 12: Knit.

Rnd 13: *K3, m1; rep from * to end (36 sts).

Rnds 14–20: Knit.

BO.

Make the second fin identical to the first.

Sew the fins onto the bottom tip of the mermaid's tail, making sure that they are both centered correctly between the hip shaping at the top of the tail.

For a more scale-like texture, try using Berroco's Zen. One ball, or 110 yards, will be enough for a tail with extra-large fins!

Seashell Top

If you don't like the thought of your mermaid going topless, you can knit a pair of "seashells" for her.

CO 2 sts.

Row 1: [K1, m1] twice (4 sts).

Row 2: Knit.

Row 3: K1, m1, knit to last st, m1, k1 (6 sts).

Row 4: Knit.

Rows 5–8: Rep Rows 3 and 4 (10 sts).

Rows 9–14: Knit.

Row 15: K2, k2tog, knit to last 2 sts, k2tog, (8 sts).

Rows 16–59: Knit.

Row 60: K1, m1, knit to last st, m1, k1 (10 sts).

Rows 61–66: Knit.

Row 67: K2, k2tog, knit to last 2 sts, k2tog (8 sts).

Row 68: Knit.

Repeat Rows 67 and 68 until 2 sts rem.

BO.

Sew two ends together and either weave in ends or tie ends in a bow. Fit over torso of mermaid.

Fauns

In classic literature, fauns were the protectors of nature. Standing in between the human world and the natural one, fauns physically embodied their two responsibilities—being both part animal and part human. This pattern will make a nice fluffy pair of goat legs, as well as a tail and some horns. You might want to knit him a nice warm scarf, too, since early writers seemed to forget to give him a sweater.

Legs and Hooves

CO 6 sts in black, or any color you would like the faun hoof to be.

Set-up round: While spacing on three dpns, knit 1 round. Join in the round.

Rnd 2: *K2, m1; rep from * to end (9 sts).

Rnd 3: Knit.

Rnd 4: *K3, m1; rep from * to end (12 sts).

Rnds 5 and 6: Knit.

Rnd 7: *K4, m1; rep from * to end (15 sts).

Rnds 8–12: Knit.

Break the yarn, leaving a 3-inch tail. Set the first hoof-half aside and make a second half with a new set of needles. Do not break the yarn for the second half. Join the two hoof-halves together by knitting from the end of the second hoof-half on the second set of needles to the beginning of the first hoof-half on the first set, similar to joining the legs in the Basic Doll Pattern on page 4.

Join the fun fur and knit 31 rounds.

Leaving the 30 sts on your needles, break off about 4 inches of yarn. Continue by working the second hoof and leg identical to the first. Do not break the working yarn for the second leg; you will be using this yarn to join the legs.

Once the legs are joined, knit 9 rounds.

Sew the crotch together back to front using the tail yarn from the first leg. Stuff the legs. Weave in the loose ends.

Tail

CO 6 sts, divide evenly onto three dpns, pm, and join to knit in the round.

Rnd 1: *K1, m1; rep from * to end (12 sts).

Rnd 2: Knit.

Rnd 3: Work as for Rnd 1 (24 sts).

Rnds 4–14: Knit.

BO. Sew the tail to the "bottom" of the faun.

Horns

CO 9 sts, divide evenly onto three dpns, pm, and join to knit in the round.

Rnds 1–6: Knit.

Rnd 7: *K1, k2tog; rep from * to end (6 sts).

Rnds 8 and 9: Knit.

BO.

Make the second horn identical to first.

Sew the horns to the top of the faun's head.

Angel Wings

Angels have been a source of comfort and inspiration to people for thousands of years. Now you can knit your very own! These impressive wings are knitted the same as a glove—with each primary "feather" knitted in the round and then joined together. Consider using a fluffy feather yarn to give your angel's wings a more authentic look.

This pattern requires one ball of Bernat "Boa" yarn, shown in Chinchilla. This yarn creates a nice, feather-like texture.

CO 6 sts. Divide evenly onto three dpns, pm, and join to knit in the round.

Rnd 1: Knit.

Rnd 2: *K1, m1; rep from * to end (12 sts).

Rnd 3: Knit.

Rnd 4: *K3, m1; rep from * to end (16 sts).

Knit every round until the piece measures 6 inches from the beginning, and move to two needles—8 sts on one needle and 8 sts on the second needle. Set aside.

Start the second feather with a new set of needles. Repeat Rnds 1–4 for the second "feather," this time knitting every round until the piece measures 5 inches from the beginning. Place the 16 sts for this feather on the first set of needles with the first feather, 8 sts on one needle and 8 sts on the second.

Start the third feather with a new set of needles. For the smallest feather, repeat Rnds 1–3, this time knitting every round until the piece measures 4 inches from the beginning (12 sts). Move the 12 sts for the third feather on the two needles with the first and second feather—6 sts on one needle and 6 sts on the second.

Next rnd: You now have three feathers on two needles—the first feather, followed by the second feather, followed by the third. Knit all three feathers together in one continuous loop, knitting from the first 6 sts of the third feather to the 8 sts of the second feather to the 8 sts of the first feather and so on. Divide the sts on the second holder needle evenly onto two needles—one with 11 sts and the second with the remaining sts. Finish knitting the feathers together, from the 8 sts of the first feather, to the 8 sts of the second feather, and lastly to the 6 sts of the third feather (44 sts).

Rnd 1: Knit.

Rnd 2: *K9, k2tog; rep from * to end (40 sts).

Rnd 3: Knit.

Rnd 4: *K3, k2tog; rep from * to end (32 sts).

Rnd 5: Knit.

Rnd 6: *K2, k2tog; rep from * to end (24 sts).

Rnd 7: Knit.

Rnd 8: *K1, k2tog; rep from * to end (16 sts). BO.

Make the second wing identical to the first.

Sew the top seam of the wing together. Sew the pair of wings onto the back of your complete doll's torso, making sure that the two wings are evenly centered, with the top of the wings sewn in at Rnd 30 of the torso. Weave in any loose ends.

Tails

If you are making an animal doll, you will want to knit a tail. After all, where would a dog be without a wagging tail to express his happiness? Or a cat, without a tail to balance her when she makes death-defying jumps? The tail pattern is simply knit in the round and sewn onto the "bottom" of the doll.

Bunny Variation: If you'd like to make a bunny doll, knit two "tails," fold them flat, and sew them to the top of your doll's head for bunny ears. Complete the bunny by adding a pom-pom for a tail.

CO 6 sts. Divide evenly onto three dpns, pm, and join to knit in the round.

Rnd 1: *K1, m1; rep from * to end (12 sts).

Rnd 2: Knit.

Rnd 3: *K2, m1; rep from * to end (18 sts).

Knit until the tail measures anywhere between 4 and 8 inches, depending on your preference.

BO.

Stuff the tail and sew it onto the body, making sure that the tail is centered correctly, between Rnds 1–9 after the leg join. The placement of the tail is the same for all animals.

Bear Variation: If you would like a shorter "bear" tail for your doll, use the faun tail pattern on page 90. You can make the tail as long or short as you want it to be.

93

Cat

Sassy, aloof, and independent—cats have a personality all their own. It's a snap to transform your doll into an adorable feline with a simple pair of pointed ears. They knit up super quick and a bit of pink intarsia will add tons of cute points, too! See the sidebar, "Working Intarsia in the Round?".

Head

If you are knitting a cat, you will want a few extra supplies. First of all, make sure you get cat-specific 18mm plastic safety eyes for your doll. Also, you can either embroider a nose on your doll's face with a back stitch, or purchase a 12mm pink triangle nose, which is worked the same way as the plastic eyes. Also consider using the protruding nose pattern on page 60.

Ears

CO 24 sts in main color (MC). Divide evenly onto three dpns, pm, and join to knit in the round.

Rnd 1: K9 in MC, join Color 1 work in Rnd 1 of chart, knit rem sts in MC.

Rnd 2: K9, work Rnd 2 of chart, knit rem sts in MC.

Rnd 3: K9, work Rnd 3 of chart, knit rem sts in MC.

Cut Color 1 and work rem of ear in MC only.

Rnd 4: *K6, k2tog, pm; rep from * to end (21 sts).

Rnd 5: *Knit to 2 sts before marker, k2tog, sm; rep from * to end (18 sts).

Rnds 6–9: Rep Rnd 5 until 6 sts rem.

BO and sew up the top of the ear together to make a point. Make the second ear. Sew both ears on top of the cat's head, making sure they are centered correctly.

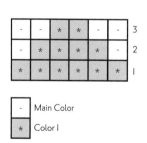

- Main Color

* Color 1

Dog

Dogs have always been a symbol of friendship and loyalty—so what better animal to knit as a doll? Using this quick and easy pattern for a garter stitch ear, you will make a floppy dog ear for your doll.

Head

If you are knitting a dog, you will want a few extra supplies. First of all, you can either embroider a nose on your doll's face with a back stitch, or purchase an 18mm brown animal nose, which is worked the same way as the plastic eyes. Also consider using the protruding nose pattern on page 60, especially if you would like to knit a pug or bulldog doll.

Ears

CO 8 sts in the dog ear color.

Row 1: Knit.

Row 2: K1, m1, knit until 1 st rem, m1, k1 (10 sts).

Row 3: Knit.

Rows 4 and 5: Repeat Rows 2–3 (12 sts).

Rows 6-15: Knit.

BO.

Make the second ear identical to the first.

You can either sew the ears to the sides of the head to make a floppy-ear appearance, or sew them onto the top of the head to make pug-like "fold-over" ears.

Bear

Ever since President Theodore Roosevelt famously refused to shoot a bear cub, the Teddy Bear has been a favorite toy of children all over the world. Why not make your own version of a timeless classic? Simply knit a pair of these trouble-free bear ears and sew them on the top of your doll's head. You could even add bear ears to the top of a hoodie or hat to make unique accessories.

Head

If you are knitting a bear, you will want a few extra supplies. First of all, you can either embroider a nose on your doll's face with a back stitch, or purchase a 12mm brown triangle nose, which is worked the same way as the plastic eyes. If you would like to knit a koala, purchase a koala nose. Also consider using the protruding nose pattern on page 60.

Koala Ears

CO 6 sts in ear color. Divide evenly onto three dpns, pm, and join to knit in the round.

Rnd 1: *K1, m1; rep from * to end (12 sts).

Rnd 2: Rep last row (24 sts).

Rnds 3 and 4: Knit.

Rnd 5: *K2, m1; rep from * to end (36 sts).

Rnds 6–12: Knit.

BO.

Make the second ear like the first.

Sew up the top of the ear together to make a round ear. Sew both ears on top of the koala's head, making sure they are centered correctly.

Mouse Variation: You can also use the koala bear ears if you are knitting a mouse doll.

Bear Ears

CO 24 sts in the ear color. Divide evenly onto three dpns, pm, and join to knit in the round.

Rnd 1: Knit.

Rnd 2: *K6, k2tog, pm; rep from * to end (21 sts).

Rnd 3: *Knit to 2 sts before marker, k2tog, sm; rep from * to end (18 sts).

Rnds 4–5: Repeat Rnd 3 until rem.

Rnd 7: Knit.

BO.

Sew up the top of the ear together to make a round ear. Sew both ears on top of the bear's head, making sure they are centered correctly.

Theodora

Bear head and ears,
p. 100
Basic Doll Pattern,
p. 2–9
Dress, p. 120

Accessories Menu

You've finished making your doll, but of course, no doll is complete without a few accessories. There are removable clothing options you can knit if you want to easily change your doll's appearance, as well as three different hat patterns, three purse variations, and even a punk rock studded belt. The best thing is that these accessories also knit up super quick, so it only takes a moment to give a little creative touch to your doll.

Sumiko

Messenger Bag

The messenger bag has become quite popular with just about everyone from students to office workers, and how could you argue? Simple and stylish, the messenger bag can hold just about everything. This doll-sized version is knitted flat, then folded and sewn together. A garter stitch strap completes the look.

Measurements: 3 inches wide × 2½ inches tall.

Bag

CO 20 sts.

Begin with a knit row, work 40 rows in St st.

BO.

Strap

CO 90 sts.

Knit 4 rows.

BO.

To sew the bag together, fold at the 15-row mark, making the front panel of the bag 15 rows and the back panel plus the flap 25 rows. Sew the 15-row side seams together and then fold the 10-row top flap over the sewn bag. Sew the ends of the strap onto the corners of the bag. Weave in the ends.

Judith

Purses

"Canvas" Tote

The recyclable, reusable, environmentally friendly canvas tote is as practical as it is fashionable. Use a natural-colored yarn to knit up this easy, trendy tote and complete the look with a simple garter stitch strap.

Tote

CO 30 sts and divide evenly onto three dpns, pm, and join in the round.

Rnds 1–15: Knit.

Rnd 16: *K3, k2tog; rep from * to end (24 sts).

Rnds 17 and 18: Knit.

BO.

Strap

CO 30 sts.

Knit 2 rows.

BO.

Sew the ends of the strap to the top edge of the bag.

Designer Purse

No matter what designer you love, you can replicate their look with this gorgeous knitted knockoff. Start with a bright color of your choice and follow with a tan and brown intarsia that mimics the fashionable grace of today's designer purses. Finish with a quick garter stitch strap and soon your doll will be wearing her new purse in style.

*	*	*	*	10
*	*	*	*	9
*	*	*	*	8
*		*		7
*	*	*	*	6
	*		*	5
*	*	*	*	4
*		*		3
*	*	*	*	2
*	*	*	*	1

* Color 1

* Color 2

Color 3

Purse

CO 30 sts in Color 1 and divide evenly onto three dpns. Place marker and join in the round.

Rnds 1–10: Knit, using Colors 1, 2 and 3, and following the chart.

When finished working the chart, break off Colors 2 and 3; the remainder of the purse is worked in Color 1 only.

Rnd 11: *K3, k2tog; rep from * to end (24 sts).

Rnds 12 and 13: Knit.

BO.

Strap

CO 30 sts in Color 1.

Knit 2 rows.

BO.

Sew the ends of the strap to the top edge of the bag.

Studded Belt

Nothing says punk quite like a studded belt, so why not make a tiny one for your rocker doll? This belt is knitted in a simple garter stitch, and completed by applying ¼-inch pyramid studs.

Variation: If you'd like a belt without all the attitude, forgo the studs!

CO 70 sts.

Knit 3 rows.

BO.

Apply the ¼-inch studs by inserting the prongs into the belt and folding them closed on the wrong side of the belt. Wrap the belt around the doll's waist. Attach it to the doll by sewing both ends of the belt together to create a continuous loop and weave in the ends.

Beanie

Beanie, toque, or cap—no section for accessories would be complete without this staple knitted hat! It's simple and easy to knit up with a bit of iconic ribbing along the brim. Remember: the beanie is not only practical winter wear, but also a trendy billboard for supporting your favorite bands or sports teams. Consider using some of the intarsia designs to express anything you want about your doll. See the sidebar, "Working Intarsia in the Round?" on page 16.

CO 64 sts. Divide evenly onto three dpns, pm, and join in the round.

Rnds 1–4: *K2, p2; rep from * to end.

Rnds 5–15: Knit.

Rnd 16: *K6, k2tog; pm: rep from * to end (56 sts).

Rnd 17: Knit.

Rnd 18: *Knit to 2 sts before marker, k2tog; rep from * to end (48 sts).

Repeat Rnds 17 and 18 until 8 sts rem.

BO. Sew the top of the hat together with a flat seam. Weave in all the loose ends.

Spice it up with a pom-pom to the top of the beanie shown in the photo.

Floppy Hat

The slouch hat conjures images of Parisian cafés and hip urban backdrops. Make sure your doll stays in vogue with this easy accessory that's knitted extra-long to give a nice floppy appearance. Add an antique button or pin for additional flair.

CO 60 sts. Divide evenly onto three dpns, pm, and join in the round.

Rnds 1–3: *K2, p2; rep from * to end.

Rnd 4: *K4, m1; rep from * to end (75 sts).

Rnds 5–26: Knit.

Rnd 27: *K3, k2tog; rep from * to end (60 sts).

Rnd 28: Knit.

Rnd 29: *K2, k2tog; rep from * to end (45 sts).

Rnd 30: Knit.

Rnd 31: *K1, k2tog; rep from * to end (30 sts).

Rnd 32: Knit.

Rnd 33: *K2tog; rep from * to end (15 sts).

BO. Sew the top of the hat together with a flat seam. Weave in the loose ends.

Swedish Ski Cap

Your doll doesn't have to be hitting the slopes to wear this Swedish-flag inspired ski cap. The hat is initially knit in the round and finished by picking up stitches for the garter stitch ear flaps. A Nordic flower motif with two-color intarsia adds Scandinavian flair. Complete the look with braided tassels on the ear flaps and on the top of the hat.

CO 64 sts in MC. Divide evenly onto three dpns, pm, and join to knit in the round.

Rnds 1–6: Knit.

Rnds 7–13: Follow the chart, repeating 8-st design eight times.

Rnds 14 and 15: Knit.

Rnd 16: K6, k2tog, pm, rep from beginning to end of row (56 sts).

Rnd 17: Knit.

Rnd 18: Knit to 2 sts before marker, k2tog, sm; rep from * to end (48 sts).

	*		*		*			7
*	*		^		*	*		6
		^		^				5
*	^		*		^	*		4
		^		^				3
*	*		^		*	*		2
	*		*		*			1

⬛	Main Color
*	Color 1
^	Color 2

Rep Rnds 17 and 18 until 8 sts rem.

BO and sew the top of the hat using a flat seam. Weave in all the loose ends. Using a crochet hook, secure 12, 10-inch strings of yarn in contrast color on top of the hat. Braid and secure the end with a knot.

Ear flaps: Pick up 10 sts on either side of the head, leaving 30 sts for the front of the hat and 14 sts for the back.

Row 1: Knit.

Row 2: K2tog, knit to last 2 sts, k2tog (8 sts).

Rep Rows 1 and 2 until 2 sts rem. BO.

Using a crochet hook, secure 12, 10-inch strings of yarn in contrast color on the tip of the ear-flap. Braid and secure the end with a knot.

Scarf

Is a scarf practical or fashionable? You get to choose with this versatile pattern, which is knitted flat using a simple garter stitch. Use fancy ribbon yarn to make a trendy accessory, or knit with wool for a cozy winter necessity.

CO 140 sts on straight or circular needles.

Knit 10 rows.

BO. Weave in the ends. Add the fringe by cutting 10, 3-inch lengths of yarn and securing them to the ends of the scarf with a crochet hook.

Ice Skates

Whether your doll is going to make a one-foot lutz or an amazing kick save, these removable ice skates are essential. Create either figure or hockey skates with this pattern that can be applied to all shoe patterns for fun, removable footwear.

A short crocheted chain sewn onto the bottom of the skate finishes the look.

CO 6 sts in either white for hockey skates or metallic for figure skates. Divide sts evenly over three dpns, pm, and join to knit in the round.

Rnd 1: *K1, m1; rep from * to end (12 sts).

Rnd 2: Knit.

Rnd 3: Work as for Rnd 1 (24 sts).

Rnds 4 and 5: Knit.

Rnd 6: Work as for Rnd 1 (48 sts).

Rnd 7: Knit.

Rnd 8: *K8, m1; rep from * to end (54 sts).

Rnds 9 and 10: Knit.

Join black yarn for hockey skates or white yarn for figure skates.

Rnds 11 and 12: Knit.

Rnd 13: K30, k2tog, pm, p2, set next 4 sts aside on a stitch holder or a needle, join second ball of yarn, p2, pm, k2tog, k12 (52 sts).

From here, the skate is worked back and forth in rows.

Row 14: Knit to 2 sts before the first marker, k2tog, sm, p2, drop the working yarn from the first ball; pick up the working yarn from the second ball, p2, sm, k2tog, knit to end (50 sts).

Rows 15–21: Rep row 13, decreasing by k2tog outside of markers (34 sts).

Rows 22–24: Knit.

Row 25: BO.

Slip 4 sts from the holder back onto the needle and knit 12 rows.

BO knitwise.

Cut a 6-inch length of yarn in either white for hockey skates or brown for figure skates and secure a tapestry needle on either end. Refer to the sidebar on page 21 in the Feet Menu for instructions on tying shoes.

With a crochet hook, chain 10 using silver or metallic yarn. Sew the ice skate "blade" onto the bottom of your ice skate.

Hoodie

At one time the hoodie was little more than simple athletic garb for warming up before a good workout. Now, it's a wardrobe must-have. Don't leave your doll out in the cold with this pattern, which is worked in the round for the sleeves and flat for the body. It can either be finished with a zipper or sewn together as a pullover. Make it extra special by adding intarsia or stripes.

Sleeveless hoodie variation: If you'd like a hooded vest, forgo knitting the hoodie sleeves. When you get to Row 32: K10, yo 10 sts, k22, yo 10 sts, k10. There you go—a quick and easy accessory to keep your doll fashionably hip!

Sleeves

CO 20 sts, divide evenly onto three dpns, pm, and join in the round.

Rnds 1–5: *K2, p2; rep from * to end.

Rnds 6–35: Knit.

Rnd 36: BO first 10 sts (10 sts).

Place rem 10 sts on a holder and set aside.

Make the second sleeve and set it aside.

Body

CO 62 sts on straight needles. The hoodie body is worked flat.

Row 1 (WS): K2, *p2, k2; rep from * to end.

Row 2 (RS): P2, *k2, p2; rep from * to end.

Rep Rows 1–2 once, then rep Row 1 again (5 rows total of 2 × 2 rib).

Beginning with a knit row, work next 25 rows in St st.

Row 31 (WS): P10, BO next 10 sts, purl to last 22 sts, BO 10 sts, p10.

Row 32 (join arms): K10, join the 10 sts from one of the hoodie arms over the bound-off sts on the hoodie body, k22, join the 10 sts from the second hoodie arm over the bound-off sts on the hoodie body, k10.

Row 33: Purl.

Row 34: K2, *k4, k2tog; rep from * to end (52 sts).

Hood

Knit 40 more rows. Use a three-needle bind off to join the top seam. Weave in ends and either sew on zipper or sew front of hoodie together.

Cardigan

Classic, chic and always fashionable, the cardigan sweater is a perfect accessory for your doll. This pattern, which is worked in the round for the sleeves and flat for the body, includes instructions for creating four button-holes for a timeless button-up look. You can always forgo buttons and sew on a zipper, too, à la Mr. Rogers.

Arms

CO 20 sts, divide evenly onto three dpns, pm, and join to knit in the round.

Rnds 1–31: Knit.

Rnd 32: BO first 10 sts (10 sts). Place rem 10 sts on a holder and set aside.

Make the second arm and set it aside.

Body

CO 70 sts on straight needles.

Rows 1–4: Knit.

Row 5 (RS): K1, p1, knit to the last 2 sts of the row, p1, k1.

Row 6: P1, k1, purl to the last 2 sts of the row, k1, p1.

Rows 7 and 8: Rep Rows 5 and 6 once more.

Continue the ribbing pattern along 3 sts at the edges of the cardigan throughout the pattern.

Row 9: K1, p1, k1, BO next 2 sts, knit to last 2 sts, p1, k1.

Row 10: P1, k1, purl to 2 bound-off sts, yo twice, k1, p1.

Rows 11–22: Rep Rows 5–10 two more times—three buttonholes altogether after 22 rows.

Row 23: K1, p1, k1, k2tog, knit to last 5 sts, k2tog, k1, p1, k1 (68 sts).

Row 24: P1, k1, purl to last 2 sts in row, k1, p1.

Row 25–35: Rep Rows 23 and 24 six more times (54 sts).

Row 36: On purl side, p10, BO next 10 sts, p14, BO 10 sts, p10.

Row 37 (join arms): K10, join the 10 sts from one of the cardigan arms over the bound-off sts on the cardigan body, k22, join the 10 sts from the second cardigan arm over the bound-off sts on the cardigan body, k10.

Row 38: Purl.

Row 39: Knit.

Row 40: BO all sts.

Finishing

Sew 3, ¼-inch buttons onto the cardigan. Sew the holes left by the arms and weave in all the loose ends.

Piercings

Making piercings for your doll is incredibly easy. Just take 2 inches of yarn (you can use any color you want; for example, you can use darker grays to simulate the look of silver metal jewelry) and thread a needle with it. Insert the needle wherever you want the piercing to be and pull it through the doll's face about two stitches away from the insertion point. Only pull the needle through about half way so that half of the yarn is on one side and half is on the other side. Tie a knot to create a loop. Pull the knot through the doll's face so that it's on the inside of the doll. There you go! You should have a nice loop of yarn that makes for an ideal piercing. And these won't even scare mom.

Dress

Dolls and dresses seem to always go hand-in-hand, like peas and carrots or apples and oranges. This is a simple, hip, halter-top style dress that you can knit for your doll. Pick some fun colors and get to it.

CO 72 sts in contrasting color (CC). Divide evenly onto three dpns, and join to knit in the round.

Rnds 1–5: *K2, p2; rep from * to end.

Rnd 6: Knit in white.

Rnds 7–31: Join yarn for Colors 1 and 2. Work in the chart.

Rnd 32: Join CC and knit.

Rnd 33: *K4, k2tog; rep from * to end (60 sts).

Rnd 34: Knit.

Join white, Colors 1 and 2.

^		^		4
				3
	*		*	2
				1

	Color 1
*	Color 2
^	Color 3

More Accessories

You can buy readymade doll accessories, such as the **glasses** on page 115, in addition to the plastic eyes or noses from local craft stores or online suppliers such as CR's Crafts (www.crscrafts.com).

Rnds 35–41: Continue working in the chart.

Rnd 42: Join CC and knit.

Rnds 43–46: *k2, p2; rep from * to end.

BO in ribbing pattern. Weave in any loose ends. Cut a 4-inch length of CC yarn and thread it into the front center of the dress, at Rnd 34. Tie it in a bow. Place the dress on the doll.

Appendix

E ven though you've reached the end of the book, it's not the end of the journey. You'll find some information here, like blank charts and extra Keeping Track forms, to help you with your next doll. You'll also find charts for numbers and letters here, too!

Knitting Abbreviations

Abbreviation	Meaning
BO	bind off
CC	contrasting color
CO	cast on
dpn(s)	double-pointed needle(s)
k	knit
k2tog	knit two stitches together
m1	make one
MC	main color
p	purl
pm	place marker
rem	remain(ing)
rep	repeat
rnd(s)	round(s)
RS	right side
sm	slip marker
st(s)	stitch(es)
St st	stockinette stitch
tog	together
WS	wrong side
yo	yarn over
*	repeat directions following * as directed

Lowercase Alphabet

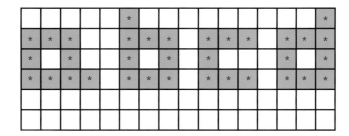

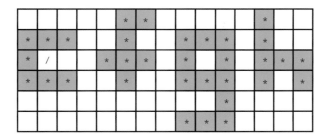

	Main Color
*	Color I
/	Duplicate stitch

			Main Color
*			Color I
\			Duplicate stitch

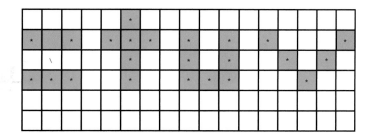

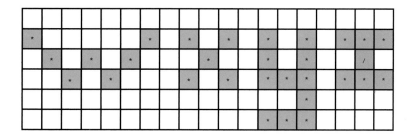

Uppercase Alphabet

Main Color

* Color I

| | Main Color |
| * | Color 1 |

Numbers

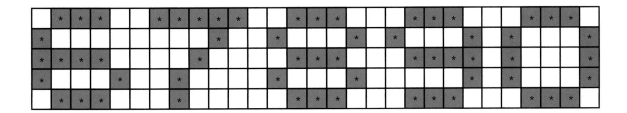

These blank charts can be used to draw your own patterns. Each chart is 20 stitches wide, which will allow you to make a pattern that will cover the chest of your doll.

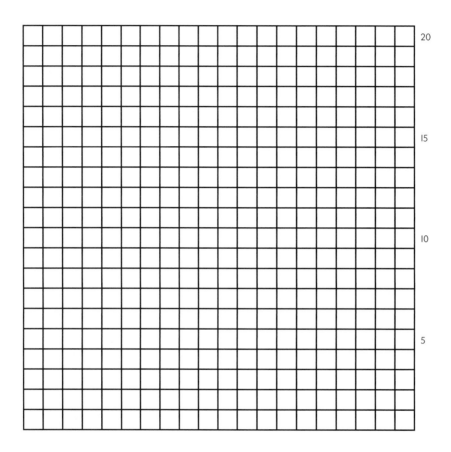

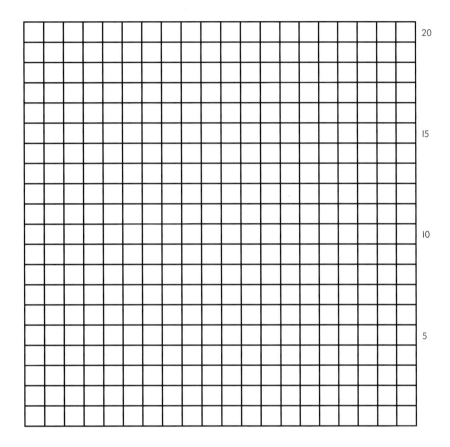

20

15

10

5

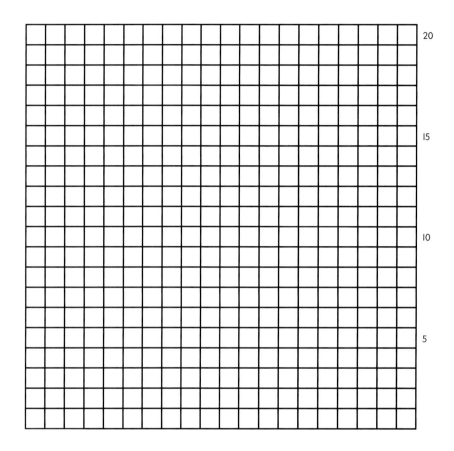

20

15

10

5

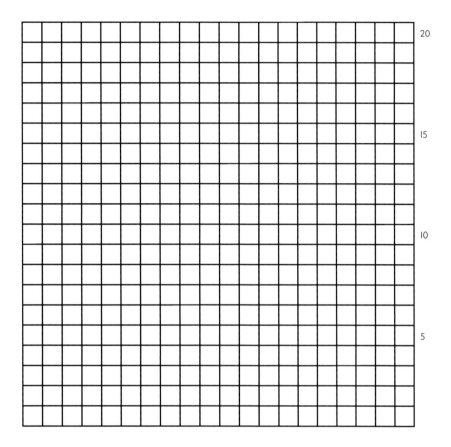

Keeping Track!

My doll is going to have...

_____ feet, found on page _____

_____ legs, found on page _____

_____ torso, found on page _____

_____ face, found on page _____

_____ arms, found on page _____

_____ extras, found on page _____

Keeping Track!

My doll is going to have...

_____ feet, found on page _____

_____ legs, found on page _____

_____ torso, found on page _____

_____ face, found on page _____

_____ arms, found on page _____

_____ extras, found on page _____

My doll is going to have...

_____ feet, found on page _____

_____ legs, found on page _____

_____ torso, found on page _____

_____ face, found on page _____

_____ arms, found on page _____

_____ extras, found on page _____

Index

About the Author

Nicki Moulton taught herself how to knit in 2002 and has been designing her own patterns for nearly as long. She first attempted amigurumi on a 12-hour flight in 2007 and has been knitting them ever since. She graduated from Northeastern Illinois University in 2010, magna cum laude, with majors in Anthropology and History. Currently she is serving in the U.S. Army with her husband, Greg.